EDWIN WHITEFIELD

EDWIN WHITEFIELD

Nineteenth-Century North American Scenery

BETTINA A. NORTON

BARRE PUBLISHING 1977 BARRE, MASSACHUSETTS

DISTRIBUTED BY CROWN PUBLISHERS, INC., NEW YORK

Published simultaneously in Canada
by General Publishing Company Limited.
First edition.
Printed in the United States of America.

Library of Congress Cataloging in Publication Data
Norton, Bettina A
    Edwin Whitefield—nineteenth-century north american scenery.
    Bibliography: p.
    1. Whitefield, Edwin, b. 1816.   2.   United States in
art.   3.   Canada in art.   I.   Title.
NC242.W54N67   760'.092'4   72-95109
ISBN 0-517-51731-0

TO THE MEMORY OF MY FATHER,

CARMEN DI STEFANO,

AND TO HIS GOOD FRIEND AND MINE,

CHARLES D. CHILDS

Contents

Acknowledgments

THE mentors and overseers of this project, to whom my first thanks are given, are Charles D. Childs, until his retirement in 1969 the owner of the Childs Gallery in Boston, and Sinclair Hitchings, Keeper of Prints at the Boston Public Library. Through the efforts of these men, the Library acquired the Whitefield diaries and other papers as a generous gift from a granddaughter, Mrs. Frances Bond, of Wellesley, Mass. The papers served as the basis of the research for this book, during my term as a Visiting Scholar at the Library.

Another prime source was the scholarly and well-documented articles in *Minnesota History* by the late Bertha L. Heilbron, formerly Managing Editor of the magazine published by the Minnesota Historical Society. Her articles were an immense help, especially since it was not possible for me to see the collection at the Society.

Many people gave the better part of a day to helping me see their holdings: Wilson G. Duprey, former Curator of the Map and Print Room at the New-York Historical Society; Avis and Rockwell Gardiner of Stamford, Conn.; Patricia Fleming, formerly of the Mariners Museum, Newport News, Virginia; August Vachon, Research Assistant in the Map and Print Room of the Public Archives of Canada; Mrs. Ignatieff, Assistant Curator of the Print Dept. of the Sigmund Samuel Canadiana Collection, Royal Ontario Museum, Toronto; Martha Hassell, Registrar of the Essex Institute, Salem, Mass.; Helena Wright, Keeper of Prints and Manuscripts at the Merrimack Valley Textile Museum, North Andover, Mass.; Georgia B. Bumgardner, Curator of Graphics at the American Antiquarian Society, Worcester, Mass.; Elizabeth E. Roth, Keeper of Prints at the New York Public Library; and Kenneth N. Newman, the Old Print Shop, New York City.

A flow of correspondence from the following people has been most helpful: Mary Allodi, Research Assistant at the Sigmund Samuel Canadiana Building, Toronto, who had written a previous chronology on Whitefield; June D. Holmquist, Managing Editor, and Dorothy Gimmestad, Assistant Head of the Audio-Visual Dept. of the Minnesota Historical Society; Ruth K. Field, Curator of the Pictorial History Gallery at the Missouri Historical Society; Mary Frances Rhymer, Curator Emeritus at the Chicago Historical Society; and Mr. Vachon.

I am also grateful for assistance from J. Russell Harper, author of *Early Painters and Engravers in Canada*; E. McSherry Fowble, Assistant Curator, the Henry Francis duPont Winterthur Museum, Delaware; Abbott Lowell Cummings, Director, and Daniel Lohnes, Librarian, at the Society for the Preservation of New England Antiquities; Jean Trudel, Curator of Early Canadian Art, National Gallery of Canada, Ottawa; William B. Osgood, Boston, Mass.; F. R. Shutte, Town Clerk, Borough of Wareham, Dorset, England; John O. Sands, Curator of Prints and Paintings, Mariners Museum; Mr. and Mrs. David Regamey, Stow, Mass.; William R. Preston of the *Brantford* (Can.) *Expositor*; Thomas Parker, Director, and Harriet Ropes Cabot, Curator, Bostonian Society, Old State House, Boston; Muriel Crossman, former Librarian at the Massachusetts Horticultural Society, Boston; Barbara Rosenkrantz, History of Science Dept., Harvard University; Nina Fletcher Little, Brookline, Mass.; Mrs. Bigelow Crocker, Fitchburg, Mass.; H. J. Swinney, Director, Margaret Woodbury Strong Museum, Rochester, N.Y.; Childs Gallery of Boston; Gerald N. Grob of Rutgers University; David Tatham, Professor of Fine Arts, Syracuse University; Earle B. Shettleworth, Jr., Portland, Maine; Peter Winkworth, Montreal; Mr. and Mrs. Jules New York City.

ACKNOWLEDGMENTS

Loeb, Toronto, Canada; Raymond C. Wright, Pittsburgh, Pa.; and the staffs of the Print Department of the Museum of Fine Arts, Boston, and the Art Department, Boston Athenæum.

Valuable editorial assistance came from Patricia and Henry Thoma of Boston. The excellent responses from many museums and historical societies helped greatly in the compilation of data for the city views. Personal thanks are due to Mary Alden Potter Meeker of Minne-apolis, Janet Andersen and Carol Messenheimer of Boston, Janet Theerman of Boston, Alva Scott Garfield, and my family, for many varieties of assistance.

Note: Parts of the text were published in *The Magazine Antiques*, August, 1972; and *Old-Time New England*, the journal of The Society for the Preservation of New England Antiquities, in Fall, 1973.

10

Foreword

WHEN Edwin Whitefield came to America in the late 1830's a revolution in methods of travel and communication was well underway. On the rivers and lakes the steamship had overtaken the sailing vessel; there were already railroads along the eastern seaboard and they were moving rapidly into the frontier midwest. And canals, following the success of the Erie, were stretching their networks into areas which still had inadequate and sketchy road systems. People and goods were in movement, and new vistas were opening. The quickening pulse of the nation was felt everywhere. Much of its energies and its strength were moving from its seacoast cities and ports into newer and yet undeveloped promising land, and with the vanguard of this movement went many of the most venturesome of our artists.

Whitefield became one of the artist-travelers who devoted a major part of his life to recording pictorially the changing scene in the cities, towns and backcountry of the United States and Canada. Known for many years as artist-lithographer and publisher of views of American cities well recorded in such source books as *America on Stone* by I. N. Phelps Stokes and Daniel C. Haskell, it remained for a store of family papers and records to reveal the multifold skills and activities of this energetic and foresighted man.

It was the good fortune of the Boston Public Library to receive not long ago from Whitefield's granddaughter, Mrs. Frances C. Bond, the generous gift of twelve volumes of the artist's diaries covering fifty years of his life from 1842 to his death in 1892 and with additional material that supplements and enriches the story of Whitefield in this country. From this primary source, from the scholarly and compre-

hensive paper by Bertha Heilbron on the artist's years in Minnesota, and from the collections of museums, historical societies, libraries, and dealers, and private collectors, Bettina A. Norton has drawn the materials that make this study possible.

From the diaries comes much that shapes the life of the artist himself—not as much as might be hoped, for there are intervals in the years, and sections that seem more revealing by the fact that they are incomplete—but the man assumes great color and character through the forthright and sometimes pungent statements of his diary notes.

He supplies running commentary on his travels by field, forest, and stream. He names major and minor exasperations afoot and ashore by boat and by rail. He names the inns and hostelries that serve him well and those that don't. His observant eye catches the everchanging bounty offered by nature, and he names those special features that bring him particular delight.

As an artist and traveler and man of strong nature and diverse capacities, as promoter, salesman, and speculator in new lands, as publisher and inventor, we come to know him well.

We see a little more of him in a photograph made about 1860 described by Bertha Heilbron in her article, "Edwin Whitefield, Settler's Artist": "Tall, thin, and wiry, with features accented by bushy sideburns and chin beard, a high forehead, and keen eyes that peered from behind metal spectacles, he looked more like a country schoolmaster than a professional artist."

Apart often from his family by his protracted trips, the shape of his home life is largely left to conjecture. Gaps appear in the sequence of years, and hope of making clear the story of the artist's two marriages and several children is dimmed by the intentional reticence of the diaries and the incomplete data now available. But the man himself appears in full focus.

As early as 1842, Whitefield was learning the practice of lithography and making views in prints based on his pencil and watercolor sketches. As a measure of success came to him, he engaged agents to act as salesmen for his city views and was constantly in touch with them. Some were good, some indifferent, some bad, and an occasional acrimonious or abrasive comment about them sparks the pages of the diary. Not only lackadaisical agents but delinquent subscribers for his prints or uncooperative publishers stirred up the old Adam in Whitefield, and on several occasions during his life he became involved in lawsuits relating to his publishing or print ventures. Some he won and some he lost.

As the years went on, and as his need required, Whitefield undertook many diverse projects in an effort to add to his livelihood. Real estate promoter, speculator in frontier lands, inventor of a drawing machine and pattern book of embroidery designs, drawing school instructor, successful publisher, talented artist and lithographer, and inveterate traveler—all these things Whitefield was, yet as a traveler he speaks best. He walked for miles through stretches of unbroken country, from village to village, constantly sketching as he went, but man of his time as he was, he saw the potential all this country had for growing towns, cities, and industries, and he engaged in a constant crusade to encourage people to move into the uncleared land and settle and cultivate it to their own profit. He knew most of the major cities and towns of Canada along the lakes and the thriving industrial centers of the United States, in the north and east and midsections of the country. He made and published views of most of these cities, and by his travels afoot, by boat, by railway, by horse or carriage, he covered many of the areas fed by our great rivers and lakes: the Susquehanna, the Ohio, the Mississippi, the Missouri, the Hudson, the Great Lakes, the Erie Canal, the St. Lawrence and their tribu-

taries. All of this is documented in his diaries.

But Whitefield, first and foremost, must be seen as an artist. He shared with Audubon, Catlin, Bodmer, Bingham, Miller, Bierstadt, the Hudson River School painters, and many others yet to come who sensed the flexing of America's muscle, the awakening of its new growth and stature. He knew, too, that change would take place, both good and bad, that it should be anticipated, and that what could be preserved of his time should be done authentically, so that future generations would see the American scene as it had honestly appeared. He devoted his late years to his pictures and books, recording the old houses of New England as he saw them, knowing that many of them would disappear even perhaps in his own lifetime—and this generation knows that many of them have indeed disappeared.

He became a proficient and prolific artist-lithographer of our great cities, leaving behind hundreds of sketches, watercolors, and a few oils, many of which are now happily located in institutions and collections often situated where the pictures were made. He must have been mostly self-trained in drawing, as he was indeed in lithography and many other talents. Although he engaged the services of several fellow publishers and lithographers in issuing his prints, and although several of his paintings were shown in exhibitions of the National Academy of Design in New York, and again in several exhibits in Canadian cities, yet Whitefield in his diaries does not mention close association with fellow artists of his time, nor does he seem to need or welcome an exchange of views or opinions with other artists. He remained alone and independent. He was his own publisher, his own promoter, his own man in every respect. And so it remains in his pictures.

Although his watercolors and drawings should reflect some of the characteristics of the English watercolor drawing school of his time, since he came from England in his twenties, yet they are sturdily colloquial and belong to no school. They are direct, quickly executed, usually lively in color and always accurate in presenting shapes and forms. Simply composed, without or with few human figures, the best of his watercolors present the scene spontaneously as the eye sees it and without the forced introduction of in-the-studio effects that are so often seen in the productions of more academically trained or sophisticated painters.

Drawings or full-scale watercolors for his many large lithographic city views are, with the exception of Brooklyn and some of the later views, no longer extant, but preliminary sketches and a few tracings of necessary detail indicate that Whitefield was a stickler for precise and accurate detail for the major architectural and topographical features of each view. Sometimes his perspective is so planned that the scene appears as a bird's-eye view—or as Harry Peters says in *America on Stone*, "Where he sat to get some of his views unless he traveled with a balloon, will remain a mystery." Yet these views tell us more about these cities in the mid-century than anything else available to us now.

In his oil paintings, at least those now available to judge, Whitefield was less proficient than in his watercolors or prints. An exception is the charming, jewellike oil of Montreal in the collection of Mr. and Mrs. Jules Loeb, Toronto, Canada. Only a few can be seen and what was said of those exhibited at the National Academy of Design is not now known. If some of his oils were included in his Canadian exhibits,

they may have demonstrated more talent than is seen in those now to be viewed, for he received both prizes and fulsome reviews in most papers dealing with his work.

He remained through his life a man of convictions intent on his main purpose and prepared to meet and cope with opposing views if they appeared.

Fortunately, now, so much of Whitefield's work can be seen in museums, libraries and private collections, including in Boston the Karolik Collection in the Museum of Fine Arts, the Print Department of the Boston Public Library and the Harrison Gray Otis House Collection (Society for the Preservation of New England Antiquities), that the artist's place can be judged fairly and dispassionately as it might not have been in his own time.

It is the devoted study and research done by Bettina A. Norton and her unremitting interest in the work of Edwin Whitefield that have made this study come to fruition, bringing alive a picture of the man and his time. To her and to Sinclair Hitchings, Keeper of Prints at the Boston Public Library, who has collaborated in the work and encouraged and aided it, full credit is due for the story of Edwin Whitefield, artist-traveler, who left a heritage of lasting worth to the generations who followed him.

CHARLES D. CHILDS

Having been nearly 20 years on this Continent, travelling
during the greater part of that time in the United States
and Canada, collecting a mass of practical information . . .
and also having, in the course of my travels, taken upwards
of two thousand Views, I am in possession of the largest
collection ever made of interesting Scenery in Canada and
nearly every State of the Union; which Views are correct
representations of the places they pourtray. These embrace
Cities, Villages, Public Buildings, Private Mansions, Scenes
of Historical Interest, Life in the Backwoods, Lake and
River Scenery, Waterfalls, &c., &c.

Edwin Whitefield, in a printed circular
issued in Hamilton, Ontario, Canada,
in January, 1854

Tintype, circa 1860, and signature of Edwin Whitefield.
Both courtesy Print Department, Boston Public Library.

THE TRAVELER

HISTORIANS and collectors of American prints and drawings are becoming increasingly interested in the accurate and direct portrayal of nineteenth-century America by its lesser-known itinerant topographical artists. Edwin Whitefield, 1816–1892, is one of these—an artist who modestly but charmingly recorded the landscapes of the Hudson and Mississippi rivers and most of the major cities of the United States and Canada from the Atlantic to the Mississippi, south to Baltimore. Forty years after the start of his career, his series of books, *Homes of our Forefathers*, with lithographed illustrations, inspired interest in the preservation of New England houses for their architectural as well as their literary or historical merits.

Whitefield arrived in the United States from England around 1837, intent on making his living as an artist. He was ultimately successful, although, like most topographical artists, he had to be constantly alert to ways to supplement his income. His inventive, industrious personality led to schemes peripherally related to the drawing pencil, but he was primarily an artist, whose energies left an incredible number of sketchbooks, watercolors, and lithographs.

The majority of lithographs belong to the following sets published during his lifetime:

North American Scenery, Faithfully Delineated, twenty-eight views published 1847.
Whitefield's Original Views of (North) American Cities (Scenery), thirty-nine views published 1845–1857, and eleven unnumbered views, primarily of Massachusetts towns, published 1866–1878.
Minnesota Scenery, Chicago, four known subjects of an intended eight, 1858.
Whitefield's Patent Combination Drawing Cards. First Series, Views

on the Upper Mississippi, eight cards, 1861.
Whitefield's Views of Chicago, seven views, 1860–1863.
Homes of our Forefathers, five hard-cover books with lithograph illustrations, published 1879–1892.

Lewis & Brown became Whitefield's first commercial lithographer in 1845, closely followed by F. Michelin and E. Jones & G. W. Newman. All three New York firms lithographed his early city views; Jones & Newman executed eight, and Michelin, four of the signed *North American Scenery* series. The firm of Endicott & Co., New York office, joined Whitefield's production with the view of Philadelphia, publishing almost all the numbered views which followed; their association continued through Whitefield's years in Minnesota.

His first American home of record was in Albany, New York. He moved to several towns on the Hudson River from 1842 to 1853, sketching landscapes and residences, and producing many flower lithographs for book illustrations. He had published almost thirty city views when a family disruption caused him to "pull up stakes and be off to Canada" in the fall of 1853. In 1855, he took a trip from Toronto to Lake Superior and, subsequently, Galena, Illinois, which he published as view number 37.

Returning to distribute the views the following year, he traveled the Mississippi River to St. Paul, and immediately became immersed in land speculation and settlement of Minnesota Territory, then the northwest frontier of the United States. He produced many watercolors shown on a trip east as agent for the Minnesota Land Agency and Kandiyohi Town Site Companies, of which he was a member. This Minnesota venture was intended as a happy marriage of his love for the lake-filled countryside with a scheme to make money as a true American promoter. He devoted three years of enthusiasm and dogged persistence, incredible energy and salesmanship to this end, but the union was unsuccessful and Whitefield moved his family in 1861 to Chicago, the fast-developing Gateway to the West. The seven views of Chicago which he drew from 1860 to 1863 are important documents of Chicago before the Great Fire of October 8 and 9, 1871.

By 1866 the Whitefield family was living in Massachusetts, near the Boston Common. Eleven more city views were executed, some in a new technique of photo-reproduction, some as bird's-eye views. The last important effort of his life was the publication of a series of volumes, *Homes of our Forefathers*, with illustrations of houses from all the New England states.

Whitefield was relentless. He contended with the laziness or incompetence of his agents and the breach of contract by his subscribers. There are few complaints in his diaries of the snow or cold weather; he once walked twenty-six miles in five hours from Brantford to Hamilton, Canada West, on a December day, in pursuit of subscribers. He was a solitary man. The diaries and journals overflow with his interests, analyses, and opinions. By inference, it is realized that he was occasionally accompanied by a wife or son. He had a sharp mind, interested in language and religion, and a sharp tongue that verged on vindictive. Literal-minded, not imaginative, he was best known for his scholarly observation. Well known in the contemporary press for his accuracy of his views, Whitefield has nonetheless been ignored by as many catalogues of nineteenth-century American art as have included him. In the Boston Athenaeum, a copy of one such catalogue has "Edwin Whitefield, 1816–1892," penciled in by the hand of a former staff member who corrected the slight. I. N. Phelps Stokes and Harry T. Peters both felt more attention was deserved; they recognized Whitefield's contribution in the large number of accurate views of American cities.[1] The Stokes collection at the New York Public Library constitutes the best-known source of his lithographs. Peters had seen less of Whitefield's work, but felt that the artist "was unques-

tionably a great deal more important" than the brief mention he was able to give.

Whitefield was born in East Lulworth, Dorset, England, on September 22, 1816; "Rogwald" was the family home in Wareham, the county seat of Dorset. Immigration records at the National Archives in Washington, D.C., have not yielded information on his date of entry into this country. Whitefield was in Troy and Baltimore in 1838 and 1839, and was also an agent of *Godey's Lady's Book* in 1838, if his first wife's account is to be believed. But a circular published by him in Canada in January, 1854, mentioning his having been nearly 20 years on the continent, suggests that he was here as early as 1837.

A picture of Whitefield and his first wife, Kate, emerges occasionally in the 1842–1848 diaries.[2] (Missing are 1844, 1845, and 1847.) Social references—to sailing parties, taking tea with friends—although sparse enough, almost disappear in later years.

The first diary in the collection at the Boston Public Library begins, "1842. Jan'. Employed, as heretofore, most of the time in teaching, and occasionally practising a little at lithography." He was commencing the technique to be of central importance to his career. By August of 1842, he had sketched two views of Poughkeepsie, "College Hill and the upper part," and "from Paltz," and was soliciting commissions from factories for pencil drawings, teaching and selling paint supplies to his students, and, interestingly, "cutting waists, &c."[3]

A house in Hudson, New York, was rented by the Whitefield family for the spring and summer of 1842, and he produced his first known professional works, the commissioned drawings of estates along the Hudson River, and watercolors of flowers. The finished drawings of houses passed into private hands, and are known to us primarily through the diaries: they pictured the residences of Messrs. Langdon and Lowman, "who commanded the best prospects," Mr. Peck's house and iron works, Haverstraw, the Newbury Regatta, and also three sketches of Mr. Roosevelt's. There are two sketchbooks of Hudson River estates, containing subscribers' names such as Washington Irving, at the Winterthur Museum in Delaware; Whitefield also included scenes of depots and tunnels along the railway.

Whitefield's drawing classes brought in a steady trickle of income which supplemented his commissions in lean years; the 1840 account book notes payment of a month's tuition by several ladies. When Whitefield arrived in Hamilton, Canada West, in the fall of 1853, after the separation from his first wife and the subsequent disruption of his family, he promptly published a circular advertising "Perspective Drawing and Sketching from Nature." During the years of his most prolific production of city views, from 1846 to 1852 and from 1855 to 1856, there are few references to classes, but they resumed again when times were difficult. A document owned by the Chicago Historical Society states that, in late 1859, "Mr. Whitefield's class in perspective drawing will meet this afternoon at four in Lopez and Pratts Commercial Room, third floor, south east corner of Third and Perry Sts. [in Davenport, Iowa]." Lest the appeal seem too narrow, Whitefield wrote:

A very common mistake is that drawing should be taught only to those who show a natural talent for it. I would ask such persons if they would teach writing to those children only who evince an aptitude for the same? If so, how few would be able to write even their names. Now Drawing is very much easier to learn than writing, that is if taught in a proper manner, and should any persons doubt this assertion their doubts will be dispelled after taking a course of lessons from Mr. Whitefield.

Over the years, Whitefield published such pamphlets as *Instructions in Map Drawing, Illustrated with Colored Plates, being a Complete Guide to That Useful Art* (1863); the Boston Public Library has the published *New England Drawing Book. Landscape Series* (1866), as well as manuscript pamphlets entitled *Tints, Drawing in Perspective,* and *Five Steps in Landscape Illustration.*

Beginning in 1845, Whitefield put on stone some of the landscapes

and residences he had sketched. Twenty-eight of these are in a series of pamphlets entitled *North American Scenery, Faithfully Delineated* at the New-York Historical Society. A trip down the Ohio River in 1846 was responsible for many of the landscapes, such as Steubenville, Ohio, the Conestoga River near Lancaster, Pennsylvania, and the backwoods of Ohio. Many were naturally of scenes on and near the Hudson: the Smith House (scene of the conference between Arnold and Andre), Haverstraw, New York; Tivoli or Upper Red Hook; and West Point. Two sketchbooks owned by the Winterthur Museum and one at the New York Public Library contain original sketches for this series.

As early as April of 1812, Whitefield had written of his determination to make a complete collection of American Wild Flowers. An opportunity was offered in the publication in 1845 of *American Wildflowers In Their Native Haunts*, by Emma C. Embury, for which Whitefield drew full-page illustrations of one or two plants, each against a backdrop of the terrain in which they would be found. On the strength of this book, Whitefield began a border for the cover of a work by Dr. A. B. Strong, *The American Flora, or History of Plants and Wild Flowers*, in four volumes, but, he wrote, "finding that there was much more work than I expected on it, I made a bargain with a young man named Rayner to finish it." Some of the illustrations accompanying the text were drawn by Whitefield. At the same time, he began eight plates of flowers for Wellman's magazine, *Illustrated Botany*, and earlier he had done five for *Sargent's New Monthly Magazine.*[4]

There is no diary for 1845, when Whitefield published his first city views of Albany, Troy, and Harrisburg. By 1846, he had published views of Newburgh and Brooklyn, and was sketching Newark. While in the midst of drawing flowers for Dr. Strong, Whitefield records that he boarded the boat for Norwich, Connecticut, to visit his children: "When I awoke found myself at Norwich, and soon after left in the cars for Plainfield, whence I walked to Canterbury (about 4 miles) and arrived there about 9 A.M. I soon found out Mr. Baker's place and the dear children were delighted to see me. They all look pretty well, but do not much like *Graham Diet*."[5] Evidently, his wife Kate was away.

The family furniture had to be removed from storage that May, and any possible mention of why it was there in the first place has disappeared with the rest of that day's entry, taking with it May 3 through 9. April 19–20 have also been cut out. Abruptly, Kate reappears to attend the State Convention of the Universalists at Newark, Wayne County, New York, to which Whitefield had been elected an alternate delegate. A son, Albert, accompanied them. During this trip Whitefield sketched Rochester, the Upper Falls of the Genesee, the first view of Niagara, and Buffalo. Albert had been left at Rochester, and, in a rare and touching family entry, they arrived back "about 10 P.M., and found Albert and his squirrel both well and sound asleep," Whitefield was actively involved in the Universalist organization and commented regularly on its promotion. The Whitefield family hosted visiting preachers and organized Sunday School meetings, and later made arrangements to buy a building in Nyack. "In the evening we had a Conference Meeting which went off very well, although there was no opposition."

From the end of March, when Kate was "galvanized"[6] till the beginning of 1850, there are no diaries; in April, 1850, when Whitefield was busy producing the Philadelphia and Salem views, Kate came home "all well." Her husband mortgaged his lithographic stones and village property in Yonkers. At this point, there emerges a second form of tampering with the diaries. In such harmless entries as "I and Kate went to New York," Kate's name is erased. Whenever Whitefield is back in Yonkers in 1852, the diary pages are missing, beginning again when he was approaching Montreal, or again in Quebec getting subscribers. Of 1853, two large segments are gone.

For the six months before Whitefield left for the trip on the Erie Rail Road through New York State in the fall, he had been at home,

gardening, working on his house, and sketching. By this time, he had published an estimated twenty-seven views of North American cities. At some point, presumably in the missing portions of the diaries, Kate and Whitefield separated. Whitefield evidently had some connections in Clinton, outside Utica, New York, for there he settled his children while he assessed upper New York, writing on October 3: "Spent all day in talking with some of the leading men here in reference to a view of their place. Did not see more than four or five, and did not meet with very good encouragement from them. I will try one day more, and if things do not look better shall probably pull up stakes and be off to Canada."

The children remained in Clinton, and Whitefield went to Canada West. There is no diary for 1854, but in December, Whitefield arranged things for the children, who arrived in St. Catherine's, Canada West, where he settled them in schools. Whitefield was boarding at the time in Paris, a short distance away. On June 21, 1855, he left for a trip to Lake Superior and the Sault that took him to Galena, Illinois, and, subsequently, Minnesota Territory.

Whitefield felt a strong allegiance to Canada. His greatest success and some of his nicest city views were in Canada (most of nos. 25–39). His travels there from 1851 on point to an extremely active, prolific, encouraging period. In January, 1854, he issued a circular "To The Inhabitants of Canada," in which he seemed ready to adopt that country, and forget his troubles in two years' travel abroad:

. . . and also having, in the course of my travels, taken upwards of two thousand Views, I am in possession of the largest collection ever made of interesting Scenery in Canada and nearly every State of the Union; which Views are correct representations of the places they pourtray. These embrace Cities, Villages, Public Buildings, Private Mansions, Scenes of Historical Interest, Life in the Backwoods, Lake and River Scenery, Waterfalls, &c, &c.

I propose to take these to Great Britain and Ireland, and by means of Exhibitions and Public Lectures, to set forth the superior advantages of

PERSPECTIVE DRAWING
AND
SKETCHING FROM NATURE.

E. WHITEFIELD, Professor of Drawing and Painting,

Proposes to give a Course of Lessons in this place to all who may be desirous of availing themselves of an opportunity seldom offered. His system of teaching is thoroughly practical, and pupils will learn more by taking one course of these lessons than by the ordinary methods in five years.

Drawing is no longer looked upon as a mere accomplishment; its practical utility in every branch of mechanics is acknowledged by all sensible men, and it should be taught in every school throughout the land. A knowledge of the principles of Perspective is the very foundation of Drawing, as Grammar is in the philosophy of language.

A very common mistake is that drawing should be taught only to those who show a natural talent for it. I would ask such persons if they would teach writing to those children only who evince an aptitude for the same? If so, how few would be able to write even their names. Now Drawing is very much easier to learn than writing, that is if taught in a proper manner, and should any persons doubt this assertion their doubts will be dispelled after taking a course of lessons from Mr. Whitefield.

He guarantees to teach all that is necessary to be known with regard to Linear Perspective in a single course of lessons; and it will be taught in such a manner that it can never be forgotten. Even should the pupil never have occasion to make use of his knowledge in after life, (a thing not to be supposed) the HABITS OF OBSERVATION *induced thereby will repay him ten-fold for the small amount of labor and time he may have spent in acquiring this knowledge.*

TERMS.

Lessons in Linear Perspective,	$3.00	Lessons in Water Colors,	$
" Shading with Pencil or Brush,	$	" Oil Painting,	$
" India Ink or Sepia,	$		$

OPINIONS OF THE PRESS.

VIEW OF PHILADELPHIA.—Mr. Whitefield has attained a wide-spread reputation by his views of other cities, and the present one adds materially to his fame.—*Phila. Sun.*

VIEW OF PITTSBURG.—Mr. Whitefield's sketch of Pittsburg cannot be praised too highly for its artistic-like finish and accuracy.—*Pittsburg Com. Jour.*

VIEW OF ALBANY.—Mr. E. Whitefield has made the best general view of the city we have ever seen. The effect of the whole is at once imposing and faithful, and is highly creditable to the skill and taste of the artist—*Albany Jour.*

VIEW OF HARTFORD.—We have seen a copy of Mr. Whitefield's view of Hartford, which for accuracy and general beauty, will challenge admiration.—*Hart. Daily Cour.*

VIEW OF TROY.—A very admirable view of our city, from a drawing made by Mr Whitefield, has just been published. This is a very handsome picture, and will instantly be recognized as a faithful portraiture of all that is within the artist's field of vision.—*Troy Daily Whig.*

VIEW OF PROVIDENCE.—Mr. E. Whitefield is certainly deserving of great praise for publishing such beautiful and accurate pictures of Providence.—*Prov. Repub. Herald.*

VIEW OF MONTREAL.—We are sure all will admit that it would have been impossible to have completed a picture more faith-fully correct than Mr. Whitefield's view of Montreal.—*Montreal Pilot.*

☞For further particulars, call on Mr. Whitefield, at

One of at least two circulars Whitefield published to advertise his drawing classes, given as an additional source of income throughout most of his career. The printed sheet containing blanks for Whitefield to alter the price and record his often-changing boarding place was probably published in 1854. 11 × 8½. *Courtesy Print Department, Boston Public Library.*

Canada over every other part of the North American Continent, in point of climate, soil, natural productions, health, state of Society, &c....

I shall probably be absent about two years, as I intend to visit every City and Town in the United Kingdom.

All persons, therefore, who are possessed of valuable information with respect to their particular localities or otherwise; those who have land for sale may address me at Hamilton until March, 1854, and afterwards at Toronto, C. W....

He did not go on the proposed trip, but his fortunes continued to go well in Canada. He received a good notice at the provincial Community Fair. This period was a high point in his popularity as an artist; after predicting that the Cobourg Fair of 1855 did not promise to be as good as the one the year before, Whitefield later wrote:

The Governor General partook of a dinner given him by the citizens of Cobourg this evening; I took five prizes, so I cannot complain.

And in Ottawa, the previous July, he had "commenced making arrangements for collecting. The views are very much liked as of course they would be."

All this encouragement led him to set up an exhibition of his own works in Toronto in 1856. Halfway through the exhibition, which lasted from February 21 to March 8,

Lady Head, Miss Head, and other ladies came to my room this morning and spent nearly an hour there. Lady Head is a very agreeable affable intelligent woman, and expressed herself much pleased with my drawings.

Lady Head and her retinue came last in a procession that started with the members of Parliament, followed in a few days by the Governor-General. The exhibit was well-attended and well-received. The diaries mention no work exhibited by name; a surmise is that it included oils of Hamilton, Montreal, and the Falls of Chaudiere, La Puce, Montmorenci, and whatever other Canadian scenery he had put to oil.

Whitefield moved continually from town to town along the St. Lawrence River: Port Hope, Kingston, Cobourg, Toronto. He sketched in Canada West the towns of London, Brantford, St. Thomas, St. Catherine's, Paris, Galt, and Adelaide. Every few days he stopped to visit his sons and daughters at their schools. The pace was dizzying. It is even uncertain which town he considered home base, if any, although a particle of evidence points to Paris.

May [1855]

Tues. 1st.
Getting my sketches of London completed and working on Mr. Lawrason's drawing.
Very pleasant weather.

Wed. 2.
Attended an auction of lots in the village of Adelaide about 25 miles W. from London, and bought two lots each 66 x 156 feet for which I am to pay $40 each in ten annual installments. This is my first speculation in Canada, in the real estate line.
Sketching &c.
Fine weather; although rather cool.

Thurs. 3.
Rode out to a Mr. Mountford's place between London and St. Thomas, and about 10 miles from the former place. Passed through a very fine agricultural country, capable however of considerable improvements especially in the way of draining and tree planting.
Took a sketch of Mr. Mountford's place which is quite a snug comfortable and rather pretty-looking establishment.
Returned to London in the evening. Raining early in the morning; fine weather afterwards.

Fri. 4.
Drawing on Mr. Mountford and Mr. Lawrason's places, sketching in the morning, and trying to get a couple of subscribers, but did not succeed.
In the evening went to Mr. Wilson's house where I spent some time. He gave me great encouragement in relation to getting something from

the Government; promised me letters of introduction, &c.

Weather clear and beautiful but quite cool for the season.

Sat. 5.

Getting ready to start on Monday. Working on Mr. Mountford's two drawings and finished them and Mr. Lawrason's.

A very beautiful day.

Mr. Wilson gave me letters of introduction to three of the members of Government at Quebec.

Sun. 6.

Took a walk in the morning, and reading &c in the eveng. Packed up in the eveng.

A charming day, though rather windy.

Mon. 7.

Left London by the 9 o'clock train, and stopped at Paris until the afternoon train, when I went on to Galt arriving there just as it was getting dark, and put up at the Queen's Arms.

Called on some of the folks in Paris about the view, and found Mr. Oliver whom I knew in Toronto has bought out Blackburn of the Paris Star.

Found also that Young and McDonnell just started a store in Paris.

The weather tolerably clear until 3 P.M. when rain came down and continued until evening.

Tues. 8.

Saw two or three persons in Galt about the view; among others Strong, who keeps a drug store (formerly of Wareham, England) who thinks I can do nothing here. I mean to try however, and flatter myself I shall raise 12 at least in Galt.

The weather was shocking bad, raining and snowing all day.

Vegetation here is not quite so forward as in London. The willows however are quite green, and elms and some other trees have a greenish look; lilacs are in full leave and nearly bursting into flower.

Wed. 9.

After calling on the papers, of which there are two, I determined to try my luck, and obtained three names to start with. Called on several others whom I did not see.

The weather very warm and beautiful.

Took several walks round the place and like the situation and appearance of the place very much.

Thurs. 10.

Sketching nearly all day, and did not see more than two persons of whom I obtained one.

A lovely day.

Fri. 11.

Sketching a little, and obtained four new names to my subscription list.

Another delightful day.

Sat. 12.

Better and better luck! I obtained five new names to-day, making 13!

This shows that it is a foolish thing to be discouraged by the fears of others.

Sketched a little. Galt will make a good view.

Very fine warm weather.

This passage is the only one in the diaries in which Whitefield talks about seeing people he had known before. It would strongly support the possibility that Whitefield first came to the United States through Canada, for entries about meeting friends or acquaintances are very rare. Indeed, other than the mention of seeing friends whom he and his first wife had known in Troy, in the diary for 1842, and occasional overnight visits with a friend, Mr. Prindle, of Brooklyn, this passage is about the only one in the diaries that does not deal only with people with whom he was involved professionally.

It is interesting that Whitefield speculated in real estate before he became involved with land companies in Minnesota, or had even been west of the Ohio. Years later, while teaching drawing in Michigan, he bought tax certificates for land in Prescott. Business deals using his art as a promotion were being pursued by Whitefield as late as his visit to England in 1888. Before the Toronto exhibition, he was visiting members of the Government, relentlessly seeking support from both the Governments at Quebec and Toronto.

Called to see Mr. Macdonald and Hon. W. Cartier, but as there was a meeting of the Council, I could not have much conversation with them. So I must defer the matter until next week.

Saw also Mr. McDonald and Mr. Spence, showed them my views, explained my plans, &c, and received pretty decided encouragement that something can be done for me; but this cannot be determined until Sir A. McNabb, Mr. Ross, &c return from England, which will be about Sepr.

Whitefield had already sketched all the major towns of Canada, and the views of Montreal and Quebec had gone into second editions. Whatever the nature of his scheme, it does not seem to have reached fruition.

The day following the Paris, Canada West, Fair on July 6, 1856, Whitefield left via Detroit and Chicago for Galena, Illinois, to distribute his view of that city. Less than two months later, he had taken up a claim on a small lake near Glencoe, Minnesota, had become a member of a speculative land company, and was subsequently to move with Lillian Stuart to the northwest frontier of the United States.[7]

From August 14 to 27, Whitefield explored Lake McLeod and the Hassan River, along the Minnesota River Valley, with McLeod, Baker, and a driver.

Sec. 17 Town 115 Range 29. Took up a claim on the small lake I saw yesterday [about six miles west of Glencoe, on Buffalo Creek].

Left our camp at 7½ A.M. and skirted the lake some time, saw immense flocks of ducks and shot 5. After this we passed other lakes and crossed splendid prairies, and at 12½ came to the Hassan River which we could not cross, and had to follow it until we came to a large and beautiful lake where we camped for the night, sleeping in the wagon....

The horses ran away last night, and the driver went after them, while we three started at 8 A.M. for the purpose of making a tour round the lake. The first thing worthy of notice was a sulphur spring at the outlet which was Hassan River, a clear and rapid stream, about 7 feet deep. Then we came to a fine grove of splendid timber and a magnificent prairie near it....

In early September he was in St. Anthony and Minneapolis, arranging another trip, and meeting with the company, christened the Kandiyohi Town Site Company. Their main purpose was encouraging settlement of their newly-created County of Kandiyohi and a future state capital of the same name. "Saw Gov. Gorman who engaged me to go to St. Peter's and make a drawing 24 inches long for which he is to pay me $200."

In the eighteen days before the party left on a second exploring trip, Whitefield sketched St. Anthony and the Fort, Minnehaha Falls, and had arranged for drawing St. Peter's. When he returned, his attention was again given to meetings of the Company, sketching, and writing articles for newspapers. The Minneapolis Territorial Fair on October 9 was "Very well attended. My gallery of views attracted a great deal of attention." An undated newsclipping in the collection at the Boston Public Library, advertising a trip east which he took in 1857, says, "These views were the chief attraction in the gallery of Fine Arts at the Territorial Fair, and their strict truthfulness was the admiration of all."

By October 13, the drawing of Minneapolis was in the mail to Endicott & Co., and Whitefield was promoting a trip east to induce settlement in Minnesota, exactly the same pattern he had followed upon arriving in Canada three years before. The Land Company met very often; Colonel Stevens, one of the most important figures in early development of Minnesota, moved to his shanty in Glencoe. Whitefield was working on the St. Peter's drawing, sketching St. Paul, copying maps of United States Surveys, writing "another article for the papers" and "trying my new paints in the afternoon on a view"

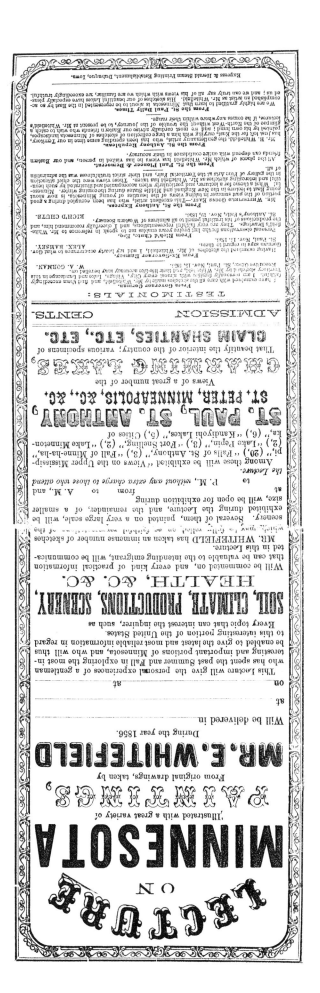

of Rapid Water which answers very well." On November 5 he finished drawing Kandiyohi at midnight.

December, 1856, was spent getting subscribers, writing and drawing for national publications, such as *Harper's* and *Leslie's Illustrated News*, and executing a copy of Minnehaha in oils. This incredible output of three months was the backbone for a promotional tour in the East on the benefits of investment in Minnesota. A colorful flyer with blanks for date and fee was printed in Dubuque, Iowa; it advertised a lecture on the excellence of "soil, climate, health &c, &c," and an exhibition of paintings "without any extra charge to those who attend the Lecture."

In contrast to the trip he failed to take to England in 1854, this less ambitious one was achieved; although there are no notes from the trip, Wilder & Co. of Boston, Massachusetts (a paper store at 26–32

The brochure which Whitefield used on a trip East in 1857 to encourage settlement of Minnesota, then still a Territory of the United States. Whitefield constantly sought and later published written comments favorable to his work. 13⅝ × 5. *Courtesy Print Department, Boston Public Library.*

Water Street) bought one share of Crow Wing West on April 15, for which they gave Whitefield a note for $200; and a favorable soil evaluation was made by the Massachusetts Department of Agriculture on a sample Whitefield brought from Minnesota. Although there is a newsclipping on the proposed trip, there are none that describe it. Whitefield had evidently left soon after the first of the year, and a proposed timetable set aside days to go to Canada, probably to visit Lillian and his children. No one had been with him on the first trip to Minnesota: "Christmas day! A dull dreary day I spent."

There is no diary for 1857, but Whitefield and Lillian probably packed up and left Paris, Canada West, on March 1, 1857, for on that day he left there a number of views, tinted and colored, as recorded in another booklet at the Boston Public Library.

A broadside published by Whitefield in Massachusetts described him as a "Dealer in Real Estate, St. Paul, M.T.," and offered all the standard services; also, "The attention of parties desiring information, &c, respecting Minnesota, will find peculiar facilities at this agency, as large and correct views of nearly all the important points open to settlement, are to be seen at this office."

A sketchbook at the Minnesota Historical Society, with two dates, shows how Whitefield spent a great deal of 1857; the sketches show camp scenes, watering places, log cabins under construction. Whitefield drew "The settler's house in the Big Woods," and "Lake Lillian from our camping ground." Whitefield pictured the men "making a grass bridge across a swamp," and "crossing a slough by hand," and the "Construction of a fence of tamarack." The dated sketches are "Diamond Lake, looking east where we camped July 1," and "Our camp at St. Cloud Oct. 4 1857." He shows Fort Snelling and the Red River train at the crossing of Sauk River twenty-two miles from St. Cloud. This was the area in which he staked out his second claim and decided to settle—the northwest corner of Stearns County, in Kandotta, on Fairy Lake, both of which he platted and named. There are many scenes of the lakes and rivers—Red, Crow, Buffalo Creek, Minnesota, Kandiyohi, Cannon.

Then Kate reappeared. Having defamed her husband to the headmaster of the school in Canada in which Whitefield had enrolled (and supported) his daughters, Kate then followed her separated husband

Advertisement published by Whitefield illustrating his personal involvement in the encouragement of land sales in Minnesota. Whitefield made other real estate investments during his travels. As in his other broadsides, referred, at the bottom, to his primary work as a lithographer. 7¾ × 5.
Courtesy Print Department, Boston Public Library.

to St. Paul. A scene ensued that was reported in the press in August, 1858, eliciting in turn a response from Whitefield, a six-column outpouring of feeling—painfully written, painstakingly exposing his affairs to public view.[8]

What had been removed from the diaries was recorded in the newspapers. A testament to their father's truthfulness was included on the bottom, signed by all the children but Albert, who was away at the time. No more was heard from Kate, and Whitefield and Lillian remained happily united.

When Whitefield became a member of the Kandiyohi Town Site Company, he became part of the great land speculation movement that had hit Chicago twenty years earlier, and was just moving up the Mississippi River. "St. Pauls and an interminable number of small places situated between it and Dubuque are starting up, and doing their best to break down everybody that invests in them," Whitefield wrote in 1856, but his own warning did not deter him. One of the Company's early hopes for encouraging settlement was for their town, Kandiyohi, to be made the state capital. A comparison between Kandiyohi, situated between Lakes Minnetaga and Kasota, and Madison, the capital of Wisconsin, also between two lakes, was a convincing argument and almost reached fruition, for, as Bertha L. Heilbron wrote, "Congress actually granted land for a seat of government at Kandiyohi, and bills calling for the removal of the capital from St. Paul to that place were seriously considered by the legislatures of 1861, 1869, 1871, and 1893. Both legislative houses passed the bill of 1869, and it was prevented from becoming law only because Governor William R. Marshall vetoed it."[9]

Kandotta was incorporated by the legislature of the State of Minnesota, and signed by Charles L. Chase, the acting governor, on February 27, 1858. The trustees were E. Whitefield, O. D. Ashley (for whom the river which flowed through Kandotta was named), and Charles Cook. Albert and Wilfred accompanied their father, for both had claims there.

Luring a railroad line through the Sauk River Valley, where the Company also had a claim, and where Kandotta was situated, was one of the objectives of an article entitled "A Winter Trip to Fort Abercrombie" and signed "Correspondence of the Press and Tribune." Linking the future of Minnesota with that of "British Canada" to the north, he stated that St. Cloud was the only major outlet north of St. Anthony, and therefore of both the Sauk River Valley in central Minnesota and that of the Red River of the North. "At this point also must cross the Northern Pacific R.R. and passing up the new State Road to Abercrombie, eventually find its way across the Rocky Mountain to Puget's Sound. Then shall we see long trains of cars sweeping down the Sauk Valley, laden with the silks of China, the lackered wares of Japan, the gold of California, etc., etc."

Twenty-eight years later, when Whitefield and Lillian returned for their first visit since they gave up frontier life, he noted that "The RR is very cheaply built in every way. The car is part passenger only, the forward end is used for express and baggage, and is as plain as it well can be." The train accommodated the Whitefields, however. "Tues. Sep. 6 / 1887 / Left Long Prairie at 830 and the train stopped at Fairy Lake for me to get off, and very soon after the whole party arrived, and we had a very pleasant Pic-Nic, and enjoyed ourselves very much returning home about 5 P.M."

Another article, written in 1857 and anonymously signed "Correspondent of the *Star*," refuted the claim of a pamphlet published by the Illinois Central Rail Road, on the bargain of buying land in Illinois; Whitefield listed the advantages of Minnesota:

The Ill. Central R.R. Company are distributing their maps and pamphlets all over the country, and doing their best to entice the people to buy their lands; and, according to their own accounts, they find every year thousands who are induced by their puffs and placards to purchase them in preference to going elsewhere.

I have long waited to see if some person better qualified than myself would take up this matter, and enlighten the public a little upon so important a subject; but I have waited in vain, and have at length resolved to make an effort towards starting the ball, and perhaps others who have more leisure and ability, may continue it in motion. I do not wish it to be understood, however, that I have little or no knowledge of the subject I propose discussing; quite the other way, I have pretty thoroughly explored both Illinois and Minnesota, and speak from personal experience....

He then quoted in entirety the stipulations, financial and agricultural, listed in great detail by the Illinois Central Rail Road, and followed it with a point-by-point rebuttal. This incredible paragraph was followed by his own mathematical calculations, and the article ends:

What! You may exclaim, is it possible that a man can save that amount—Six Thousand Dollars—in six years, by buying 80 acres of government land in Minnesota instead of the same quantity of the I.C.R.R. Co.? Yes, my friends, it is a positive fact; as certain as that five and five makes ten. What do you think of it? [Whitefield felt he hadn't exhausted the subject.] This is merely a beginning, a sort of introduction to the subject. For the present, however, we will rest, and, perhaps, in a few days take up the matter more at length.

This seething, intelligent, sarcastic, restless man was an entrepreneur; he saw the advantages of industrial development and filling the countryside with people. He was intensely interested in making money, and yet he had chosen the site for his home as an artist, primarily on the basis of its beauty and proximity to a body of water, which he loved. It was indoors on a rainy day that he composed these articles, researching on soil, climate, railway development.

It took Whitefield almost a year to clear enough land, construct a log house and hotel, and collect the necessary equipment and livestock to live five days from the nearest active town. He finally moved Lillian and their infant daughter, Lillie, to Kandotta in October, 1858, noting "Home is found at last! Kind Providence be thanked!" Whitefield spent the month of December tracking down household

goods that came in by boat, collecting money in St. Paul and St. Anthony, and buying a stove and sending it by team to St. Cloud. He also found some farmers with whom he discussed a corn sheller, evidently another scheme of his, and spent another Christmas away from his family. On December 27, he left St. Cloud with flour, meat, and the stove, taking three days to reach the shanty of a man named Ober. The sleigh broke on the way. On the night of December 31 they reached "the James'—Could not persuade any one in the house to open it for us so we were fain to make our bed in the corn-crib, and a pretty cold time we had of it."

On another trip, "Left St. Cloud after getting some groceries &c about 10 A.M. the ox teams having left three hours before. Got on very well until evening, when just after it got dark and I was within half a mile of Jacob's Prairie my sled broke down and my load was all pitched into the road. There was nothing for it but to unhitch the horse and ride him to Jos. Hopper's about half a mile beyond Jacob's Prairie where I might hope to get some help. It was very dark and I found it pretty difficult to keep the road but I found the place at last and on knocking at the door who should open it but Albert. It was certainly singular that we should both meet where neither of us expected to be as I supposed he would be found at Wakefield's a mile beyond.Cold Spring but as the oxen had given out he was obliged to stop at the first house he came to, and here we all were. He and I then after taking a cup of warm coffee went back and got a Dutchman at Jacob's Prairie to take our load to his house. We then went back to Hopper's pretty well tired out and pretty soon got to bed."

There was little time for drawing or writing, but he did do some watercolors of Kandotta, and wrote two articles for the *Chicago Press and Tribune.* "A Winter Trip to Fort Abercrombie," quoted earlier in regard to luring the railway, is on the face of it an explorer's journal of a week-long trip. Actually, it is a shameless glorification of Kandotta by its sole occupant masquerading as a stranger-journalist. The excuse was an overnight stop caused by a disabled sleigh. Several members of the party took a walk while the sleigh was being repaired. "At first we crossed a tract of undulating prairie, interspersed with pretty groves and scattered trees, towards a fine sheet of water, called Fairy Lake, which, although now covered with ice, we could well imagine to be worthy of all the praises which we heard bestowed upon it by the settlers here." One member who stayed indoors made many notes on the climate, soil, and crops of central Minnesota, pronouncing them all good. All in all, the Sauk River, into which flows the Ashley River of Kandotta, "meanders through the finest country in Minnesota—a country possessing everything which the new settler can desire: prairie, timber and meadow land interspersed in such an advantageous manner that scarcely a claim can be found which does not possess all three."

In the second article, "From the Mississippi to the Red River of the North," written to correct "the omissions of the first," Whitefield discussed the price of land, the U.S. government plat numbers, post offices (one had been established at Kandotta in 1858). Still keeping up the deception, he wrote, "I cannot give the above particulars except for Kandotta; where, as we staid the longest, we obtained the greatest information. On referring to my note book I find that Kandotta is in section 27, township 127, north range 34."[10]

Whitefield left Kandotta for two months in May and June, 1859, traveling to Springfield, Illinois, and St. Louis, where he received several commissions to sketch Capt. Brown's residence and the steamboat he was building, and Belcher's Sugar Refinery. The steamboat was put on stone on June 17. He took a second trip down the Mississippi in October, stopping at Hannibal, Quincy, and Dunleith (now East Dubuque).

On a visit to Chicago in 1858, Whitefield had arranged with Rufus Blanchard, publisher, for a series of lithographs, *Minnesota Scenery*; during ten days in April and May he drew four views on stone. In 1860 Whitefield was involved in another project with Blanchard, a center illustration for a broadside of candidate Lincoln as a flatboat-man on the Mississippi. His one other lithograph of political interest was the *Republican Wigwam*, published by McNally & Co., Chicago.

Whitefield also drew the first of his street views of Chicago, *View of Illinois and Michigan Central Depot, &c*, for D. B. Cooke & Co. When he gave up living in Kandotta in 1861, it was natural to move to Chicago to finish the series. A trip later that year up the Rock River Valley into Wisconsin, to Fox Lake and on the Wisconsin River to Portage City, then west to La Crosse on the Mississippi, proved unfruitful, and Whitefield returned to Chicago. On June 7 he began work on the Tremont House. A second daughter was born in August. The Whitefields, trying a new venture, opened a store and "took in the astonishing sum of 11 cents!" He remained in Chicago for two more years, completing seven views. Another trip in 1863 produced an article for the Chicago *Western Railroad Gazette*, a newspaper distributed free of charge to hotels and railroad lines throughout the states: "Chicago to Cincinnati, via Chicago Cincinnati Air Line; Towns and Cities along the Route, &c." The thousand-word article is observant, literal, crammed with facts, and full of his opinions. The tone is lightened a bit by his sarcasm: "In fact, for anything of interest worth looking out for, a man might about as well shut his eyes for the first 100 miles of this road."

Whitefield's artistic successes had taken a decided downhill turn. For seventeen years he had been at work sketching several city views simultaneously, traveling and soliciting subscriptions continually. In Canada, he had been received very well, and seems to have extracted as much out of the area as possible for an artist. Then followed a period of high hopes and great energies devoted to a cause. Regarded as the "Eastern Yankee," "The Great North American Artist," the "Gentleman settler," he occupied a position apart from the other explorer-settlers, which he no doubt enjoyed. They looked upon him as the literate member of the group, who could add the unique aspect of pictorial representation of a land they felt was all any man would desire. Whitefield wrote articles and showed his watercolors, but no one came to live. Those who did not make it to Minnesota by the time the nation became embroiled in its Civil War were critically detained. For many others, the land was an investment, and they had no intention of leaving the East.

It is difficult to say what influence the Civil War had on Whitefield or his career. He and Lillian started east in 1863, but detoured north at Lake Champlain, and went to Canada. There is almost nothing for the next two years. The publications, *Instructions in Map Drawing*, published in 1863, and the *Patent Topographical Business Directory*, Montreal, C.E. copyrighted in 1864, with "patents applied for in Canada, the United States, France, &ca," indicate that he was primarily publishing maps and teaching drawing to make a living. It seems safe to say that he did not publish another lithograph until the *View of the Public Garden & Boston Common* in 1866.

In June, 1866, the diary starts again in Boston; he was back at the familiar routine—sketching Roxbury and Boston, and contemplating a view of Charlestown, where he saw the Mayor who subscribed for his view.

All July, he worked on fruit and flower pieces, patented a method of stamping embroidery patterns, and was again trying to persuade officials of some plan:

After dinner went to Swampscot, 3 miles from Lynn and saw the British Consul on a certain subject (Fenianism) which we talked over for some time, and finally he thought my plan a good one, and wrote a letter of introduction to the British Minister at Washington, advising me to go on as soon as possible. Remained with him about 3 hours.

Nothing seems to have come of his schemes.

There are no diaries extant, possibly even written, after 1866, with the exception of those for the two trips away from home for any length of time: in New York in 1882–1883 while he was drawing the Cypriote Collection given to the Metropolitan Museum, and a more sporadic collection of notes from a trip to England and Scotland in 1888–1889.

A few copyrights are the only clues to the years between 1866 and 1870, when he bought a house in Reading, Massachusetts. He worked on eleven more city views, which, with the exception of the first two, the *View of the Public Garden . . .*, and *Fitchburg, Mass.*, are different in character from the earlier views. The careful portrayal and architectural accuracy are still present, but the views are lacking the embellishments of foreground trees and superficial activity. There are no known hand-colored prints, except that of the Public Garden. All but the two views of *Portsmouth, N.H. On July 4th, 1873*, are of towns in Massachusetts.

For the last twenty years of his life, Whitefield devoted himself to a series of books on New England houses, called *The Homes of our Forefathers*:

The Homes of our Forefathers in Massachusetts, three editions, 1879 and 1880.
The Homes of our Forefathers in Rhode Island and Connecticut, 1882.
The Homes of our Forefathers in Maine, New Hampshire, and Vermont, 1886.
Homes of our Forefathers in Boston, Old England, and Boston, New England, 1889.
The Homes of our Forefathers in Massachusetts, New Edition, 1892.

They represented a great deal of travel and research, and are the facet of his career by which he was most generally known.

Fortunately, the sketchbooks, as well as many working drawings and tracings, have survived, and are at the Boston Public Library and the Society for the Preservation of New England Antiquities.

As Whitefield's obituary pointed out, he was more than a nostalgic antiquarian.[11] A page from a proposed journal written about Quebec illustrates his flexible but strongly critical outlook:

THE HOMES
OF OUR
FOREFATHERS

BEING A COLLECTION

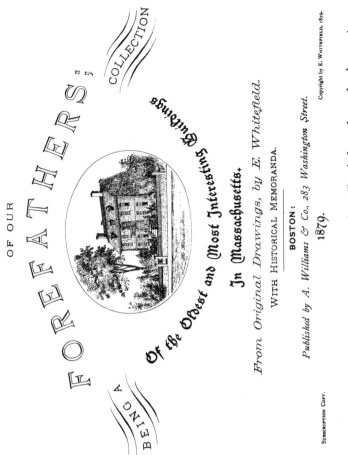

Of the Oldest and Most Interesting Buildings

In Massachusetts.

From Original Drawings, by E. Whitefield.

WITH HISTORICAL MEMORANDA.

BOSTON:

Published by A. Williams & Co., 283 Washington Street.

1879.

SUBSCRIPTION COPY.

Copyright by E. Whitefield, 1879.

Title page of the first volume of *The Homes of our Forefathers*, devoted to houses in Massachusetts (published in 1879). Although Whitefield drew almost every illustration for this series "from nature," several important residences had burned or been torn down before he began the project. The Hancock House, torn down in 1863, was one. *Photo courtesy The Society for the Preservation of New England Antiquities.*

It would seem that these French have no more invention than so many birds that build their nests after the same pattern from generation to generation. . . . It is true that at Rivere [Rivière] du Loup there is some little show of improvement; but even there they having made one step forward are evidently afraid of advancing another.

A book on which Whitefield worked in New York constantly for six months in 1882–1883 was an *Atlas of the Cesnola Collection of Cypriote Antiquities* for the Metropolitan Museum in New York. The collection had been sold to the Museum by General Luigi Palma di Cesnola, before he became their first paid director. Whitefield had drawn fourteen sheets of vases and fifty bronze objects before the contract for the work was signed with the Heliotype Printing Company of Boston,[12] and he wrote in his diary, "Mr. Edwards came to-day and at last gave me the AGREEMENT. I am thankful as now all doubt is at an end." Edwards and Cesnola periodically expressed pleasure at the work. Whitefield drew the remaining bronzes, then fifty gold objects, and some glass; he received $800 by May, and set up a tight schedule to finish the work by August.

An atlas of the collection was published, but there is no illustration attributed to Whitefield. There is absolutely no record of him at the Metropolitan Museum in the Print Department or the Archives. Correspondence from the General indicated satisfaction with the drawings themselves, but the Heliotype process was unsuitable. Whitefield complained to someone at the Museum that Edwards' chief interest was in doing the book as cheaply as possible, and that he wanted no part of the Company under those conditions. Then the Heliotype Printing Company failed. A carefully penned title page at the Society for the Preservation of New England Antiquities has the words, "*The Cesnola Collection of Cypriote Antiquities, Drawings by E. Whitefield*, 1891," marching in vertical procession into the foreground, and the copyright is registered at the Library of Congress. A letter from Isaac Hall, secretary at the Museum, to Whitefield in March, 1892, probably refers to the subject,

telling the artist flatly that it is too late for anything to be done for him and wishing his family well.

Bertha L. Heilbron wrote of a bound volume of thirty-seven original watercolors of Minnesota and Wisconsin lake and river scenes, with text and maps, now in the collection of the Minnesota Historical Society: "It bears the stamp of a book which never found a publisher."[13] In the Library of Congress are titles which never found a book. In his later years, Whitefield thought of publishing two books related to subjects dear to him throughout his life—religion and language. *The Bible—Its Own Interpreter* was registered on March 19, 1884; *The English Alphabet Revised and Improved*, on November 16, 1889. Manuscripts for both these books are in the Boston Public Library, but, like the *Atlas for the Cesnola Collection*, they were never published.

Maps were another of his projects. In addition to the publication of *Instructions in Map Drawing*, copyrighted in 1863, he drew maps of Ottawa, Montreal, Toronto, Buffalo, and Back Bay, Boston, Massachusetts. In 1850, he was working on a map of West Chester and selling subscriptions for it in Yonkers. Montreal, Chicago, and Buffalo were published. From statistics he had gathered in fifty years of sketching, he planned *Growth of Cities in the U.S. From the First Census 1790 to 1890 Inclusive*.

A sideline of Whitefield's career which was more successful was the invention of a method for stamping embroidery patterns on cloth, which he called Notosericum. (Latin, *noted on silk*). He patented this in 1867 and Whitefield's Patent Fluid for transferring designs in 1886. Although Whitefield himself is listed in only one Boston City Directory from 1867 to 1871, his wife is registered during these years as an Embroidery Stamper, 28 Winter St.; there were approximately ten ladies in Boston so engaged at the time.

Whitefield and Lillian returned to England and Scotland, the countries of their birth, in 1888. Their daughter Lillie and her husband Donald Ramsay saw them off in Boston on May 26, and they arrived in Liverpool on June 7. Whitefield kept track of the latitude, longitude, and distances traveled daily, noting, "The Capt'n took no observation to-day as he knew where he was I suppose." Comments from several sketchbooks indicate the tone of a guide he thought of publishing on his return: "London people are a set of sharks." ... "Pretty women / Have not seen any in London / a few in Leamington, and one on the cars going to Manchester." ... "Cabbages not half-grown

each / 2, strawberries 2/6 a small quart". ... "The Londoners are the most driving go-a-head people in the world. The New Yorkers can't hold a candle to them. ... Be sure in making a bargain that you ask if there are any extras. If not you will be surprised when you come to pay your bill."

Scotland was much more pleasant. "When they receipt a bill here they always put 'with thanks'." ... "Post Office in Glasgow / Every accommodation; far beyond the Boston P.O." ... "Chairs, tables, furniture of every description, strong, will last 3 times as long as that made in the U.S."

Whitefield visited his old school friends; the schoolhouse itself, in Wareham, had been torn down. A letter to him from Hamilton, Ontario, dated December 20, 1890, says:

I was very glad to hear of your visit to the old places, and should have been pleased to hear of your impressions on seeing them after so long an absence. You saw your old house "Rogvald" of course, and very likely mine. I wonder if I ever shall. ... I remain My dear Mr Whitefield
Yours very truly S. W. Townsend

The Townsends were living in Toronto when Whitefield was active in Canada; he mentioned visiting them often. Except for a Mr. Prindle in Brooklyn, possibly the publisher of *Williamsburgh, L.I.*, in 1852, Whitefield's only friends mentioned more than once in the diaries are the Townsends, a link to England.

There are several highly outspoken letters in the collection at the Boston Public Library, which one would assume satisfied his rancor upon being set down on paper, but which were never actually mailed.

Mr. Moody———
You had better give up your present business as soon as possible, for you are nothing but a *QUACK* in Religion. The fact is you understand Christianity about as much as one of the Bulls of Basham, or Balam's ass understood the Law of Moses. ... How can you be such an ignoramus,

Boston, April 23, 1877

Moody? Why you are as blind as a bat. Go and get a pair of Common-Sense Spectacles, then read your Bible, and it may be you will understand it better.... Fare you well Moody. I have no ill will against you. You are to be pitied, because you don't know any better. Be sure to have all the Blood you have sprinkled around the Tabernacle so liberally, well scrubbed up before you go.

The letter was evidently directed to D. L. Moody, evangelist and founder of the Northfield Mount Hermon School.

Another letter, addressed to the editor of the *Transcript*, denounced throwing around poisoned food to kill the sparrows. Whitefield would like to propose getting rid of "Robbins" instead:

A friend brought a gun and killed 39 in two days.... It appeared to me that for each and every bird he killed about a dozen came to his funeral.

The letter was published in the *Transcript* July 22, 1890.

Only once in the diaries does he mention his parents: "Rec'd letters from my Father and Mother who are about as usual." A few letters to members of his own family written from England in 1888–1889 have survived:

My Dear Lillie
You will find, accompanying this, a letter from your Mother, which as you may suppose was for her a great effort. She is foolishly sensitive, and thinks her writing very bad, and the pen was a bad one, but I know she would be a very pretty writer if she would only practice a little more. So you must value it very highly, as rare articles bring a high price....

The house and land in Reading, Massachusetts, which the Whitefields owned from 1870 to 1888, the longest period in one location, were sold before they went abroad. When they returned, they lived for a time in Roslindale, Massachusetts, then boarded with their widowed daughter Lillian in Dedham. In all the years of traveling, Whitefield spent many Christmases away from family. He died at the home of his daughter on Christmas night, 1892.[14]

Whitefield bequeathed everything to his wife, Lillian—"all property whether real or personal, of which I may be possessed at the time of my death whether such property may be found in the State of Massachusetts or elsewhere"—except for the sums stipulated to his children, and three oil paintings, which were to go to Donald Ramsay, his son-in-law; Elliott D. Robbins; and George Capen, who became a son-in-law before Whitefield's death. All the grandchildren were to get sets of the books.

The bequests to his children were small, but most striking is the fact that he did not know the residence of his oldest son, Edwin A. (presumably Albert), nor the married names of any of his daughters from his marriage to Kate:

To Lillian K. Ramsay   Ten Dollars
To Mabel J. Whitefield   Twenty-five Dollars
To Edwin A. Whitefield (should he be living)   five Dollars
To Wilfred J. Whitefield   Twenty-five Dollars
To my daughter Cordelia (I don't know her married name)   Five Dollars
To my daughter Constance (I don't know her married name)   Five Dollars
To Rogvald Whitefield,   Five Dollars
To my daughter Edith (I don't know her married name)   Five Dollars

The executor's inventory (Lillian was the executrix) listed $493.50 in cash, of which $320 was in assets from the books, *Homes of our Forefathers*, and no real estate. The land and house in Reading, "Beard Orchard," were sold in pieces to his daughters Lillian and Mabel, between 1882 and 1888. According to an article, "The Complete History of Kandotta," printed in the *Sauk Center Herald* in 1928, Mr. Whitefield's daughter Lillian, later Lillian Ramsay, probably received the land before the death of her father. Whitefield and his wife had visited Minnesota in 1887, and a great deal of surveying was done, presumably for disposition of the land. At any rate, his only assets at the time of his death were the unsold volumes of *Homes of our Forefathers*.

Plums and White Grapes. / *Painted when E. Whitefield was a young boy. Watercolor, 4⅜ × 5½. Courtesy Print Department, Boston Public Library.*

THE ARTIST

I

$\mathcal{T}$HE earliest known Whitefield watercolor is a miniature at the Boston Public Library, *Plums and White Grapes*, "Painted when E. Whitefield was a young boy," presumably around the time he first arrived in this country at age eighteen or nineteen. A pencil sketch, "Bridge Over the Canal at West Troy [now Watervliet] / The first sketch I ever made from Nature / Drawn by E. Whitefield, 1840," owned by Mrs. L. E. Crossman, Danvers, Mass., a beginner's effort, stands in strange contrast to a sketch signed and dated January, 1837, that is similar to, or possibly is, a view of St. Andrew's Church, in East Lulworth, Whitefield's birthplace. From the level of skill in drawing and composition, the latter, in the collection at the Society for the Preservation of New England Antiquities, strongly suggests that Whitefield copied a drawing book illustration. However, five pencil drawings in the New York Public Library, all dated June, 1841, show a year of solid development. He had acquired a sense of perspective, good rendering of distance, and a sure and delicate line, characteristics which consistently marked his subsequent work.

Although Whitefield was essentially self-taught, he looked for guidance in the works of well-known contemporaries. There are eight previously unidentified pages from a drawing book of J. D. Harding in the Whitefield papers; he seems to have taken his own advice: "Obtain Harding's Elementary Art. Pub. 1835." Whitefield himself might have written such a passage as this by Harding:

To those who are seeking a short road to Art, it may be unpalatable to be told that none can be shorter than that which knowledge makes short; and that there are no by-paths by which idleness and indifference may find their way to a goal, which is only to be reached by industry and intelligence. [15]

The title-page of Part I of *Lucas' Progressive Drawing Book* has a trompe-l'œil still-life of a landscape with watercolor brushes, an aquatint by J. Hill after E. Van Blon; Whitefield executed a similar painting, owned by Mrs. Bertram K. Little, Brookline, Massachusetts, adding a vase of flowers and a pen-knife. It is a very unusual picture, for Whitefield rarely painted still-lifes. Perhaps also it was J. Hill's aquatints after paintings by W. G. Wall in the *Hudson River Portfolio* which inspired Whitefield's series. He may have seen these books when he was in Baltimore in 1838.

During the early 1840's, Whitefield began work on his first published lithograph series, *North American Scenery, Faithfully Delineated*, twenty-eight views of scenery around New York, Pennsylvania, Ohio, and Connecticut. Of those in which the lithographer is identified, eight are by E. Jones & G. W. Newman, and four by F. Michelin. All are approximately 6" x 9", with the title centered below the image. There are two styles of lettering, and some have a tintline border. A letter in the Whitefield papers, written to a granddaughter in 1939, mentions recently acquiring them, "with the addition of text by John Keese, Esq. The first is dated January 1847, & the 7th Aug. of the same year, & that was apparently, from a note, the last one issued." Three views from the Stokes list published in *American Historical Prints, Early Views of American Cities, &c.*—"Steubenville?," "Fountain Park, near Philadelphia," and "Tivoli, or Upper Red Hook, N. J."—belong to this series.

Although Whitefield by this time had fully developed his skill with the pencil, this was not so with the lithographic crayon. The production of this series is uneven. His handling of volumes of water, especially waterfalls, is awkward and unconvincing. Perspective and dis-

Trompe-l'oeil still-life, signed on the knife-blade "Whitefield. Feb. 1844." Watercolor, 8 × 9½. Private collection.

tance are well rendered, however, and the successful ones, such as *Part of Steubenville*, *View on the Conestoga*, or *Otsego Lake*, are delightful.

The timid execution of some of his earliest landscapes is noticeably absent in the handling of his early flower watercolors and lithographs. Whether or not Whitefield studied law and medicine in England,

which seems doubtful considering his age when he arrived in this country, it seems he early acquired some formal knowledge of botanical painting. His flowers are delicate, clear in color, painted with a minute and steady brush. *Fairy Flax & Crow-foot Geranium*, from *American Wildflowers In Their Native Haunts*, shows leaves so carefully painted that the tiny veins are indicated by the absence of paint.

34

Part of Steubenville, Ohio, one of twenty-eight lithograph illustrations from North American Scenery, Faithfully Delineated . . . Lithograph, 6 × 9. Courtesy of the Print Room, New-York Historical Society.

His very early watercolor, *Plums and White Grapes*, shows the genesis of this technique. Whitefield's ability was recognized by the judges of the American Institute of New York, who awarded him a medal for the best painting of fruit in 1842.

American Wildflowers In Their Native Haunts, published in 1845, was a step toward realization of the desire he expressed in 1842, to

"make a complete collection of American Wild Flowers." The backgrounds of the lithograph illustrations are left uncolored, the flowers are hand-colored. The lithography was done by Lewis & Brown, who also printed Whitefield's first city views. Since the delightful and well-executed scenes each provide sunny valleys, plateaus, river beds, and shady nooks, they are more decorative than informative. But the

35

Fairy Flax, and Crow-Foot Geranium.—Passaic Falls, New Jersey, third of the twenty illustrations by Whitefield for *American Wildflowers In Their Native Haunts,* published simultaneously in New York and in Philadelphia by G. Appleton & Company, in 1845. Hand-colored lithograph, 9½ × 7¼. Photo courtesy Massachusetts Horticultural Society.

botanical descriptions with Latin names, and the paragraphs on background scenery, written by Whitefield, are quite explicit. Mrs. Embury's contributions were emotion-draining tales of moral maidens and secret loves, and occasional spouts of poetry. As the Preface reveals,

The botanical and local descriptions accompanying the plates, have been furnished by the artist, Mr. E. Whitefield. The verses, beginning "she sleeps," inserted in "Love Beyond the Grave," were presented for publication by a friend. With these exceptions, the author alone is responsible for every thing in the volume which has not the name of its writer affixed....

Brooklyn, September, 1844.

Whitefield supplied the illustrations for several other books published in the 1840's.

Aside from the sketchbook from his trip on the Erie Railroad in 1853, the earliest watercolors known at this time to have been produced in any number were of scenes in Canada. For most of his early career, Whitefield seems to have looked upon his watercolors as sketches or preliminary works—studies for lithographs or occasionally paintings in oil. The Royal Ontario Museum owns many fine watercolors and wash drawings, and sketchbooks also, from his two periods in Canada, 1854–1856, and 1862/3–1864/5. The very sensitively sketched and colored *From Durham Terrace/Quebec* might have been intended for lithographing, but *Among the Adirondacks, N.Y. In Early October* is a finished watercolor, and probably dates from the mid-1860's. *Chapel at Tadoussac,* signed and dated 1863, was conceived as a finished work.

The Museum of Fine Arts in Boston, Massachusetts, and the Minnesota Historical Society, St. Paul, Minnesota, record the Minnesota adventure in sunny, appealing pictures, *Cooking a Camp Meal, Claim Shanty near Glencoe, Minn., Discovery of Fairy Lake—A Lake! A Lake! Hurrah!* The latter became the subject of one of Whitefield's *Minnesota Scenery* lithographs, along with two views of Minnehaha Falls and one of Kandotta. Another landscape, *McLeod Lake,*

60 m. w. of Minneapolis, with a later note, "now Marion Lake," probably came east with Whitefield in 1857 and was seen by Bostonians who attended his lectures on the charms of land in Minnesota. One hundred years later it is back in Boston. One of the most delightful was a labor of love, the very detailed, very picturesque watercolor of his home, *Kandotta, M.T. in Oct. 1857*. Another watercolor in the Boston Museum, untitled, shows steps leading up a bank to three tents and a log house. It is Kandotta. By October, 1857, the steps had been replaced by a dirt road, three buildings replaced the tents, and a flagpole was up. The Minnesota Historical Society also owns a watercolor of Kandotta painted one month later. The Chicago Historical Society owns a larger one, approximately 8" x 10", poignantly entitled *Kandotta in 1859 / Before it was burnt by the Indians*.

A delightful project which emerged from the Chicago years was his Mississippi series of Patented Drawing Cards, eight interchangeable scenes along the Great River. These combined Whitefield's artistic skills with the prevalent Victorian drawing-room pastime of playing-cards. (The idea was not original with Whitefield; there are five English Neo-classical scenes in aquatint in the exhibition case of children's toys at the Society for the Preservation of New England Antiquities.) From the amusing, gaily assembled circular advertising the cards, to the watercolors and lithographs themselves, they are charming. Whitefield pleasingly varied the foreground and background in each self-contained scene, and yet they interconnect well.

There are several other sets that exist in wash drawings only, as far as is known at this time. Avis and Rockwell Gardiner of Stamford, Connecticut, have in their very extensive collection two interconnecting Hudson River scenes and three interconnecting European(?) landscapes.

The Gardiners also own a fine example of a large finished watercolor by Whitefield, a pastoral view of *Hingham, Mass.*, in the distance beyond a swampy pasture with cows.

Whitefield intended at least two series of chromolithographic views

in the late 1870's and 1880's. The known prints were quickly and rather carelessly executed, and are less satisfactory than the early lithographs, which, although sometimes awkwardly drawn, are nonetheless more detailed and more charming. A great deal of Whitefield's appeal is in his line, and the deliberate diminution of it in this attempt at chromolithography accounts for the relative lack of appeal of this series.

Whitefield did little commissioned work for which he did not conceive the idea or direct the seeking for subscriptions. The lithographs he drew for the Lincoln-Douglas Presidential campaign of 1860 were probably commissioned by the Chicago publishers; the illustrations intended for the publication of General Luigi Palma di Cesnola's collection of Cypriote Antiquities were commissioned through the Heliotype Printing Company of Boston. But the two major productions of Whitefield's career—the vast number of city views and the

Wreck of the Swallow. / The only correct View. / As seen on the morning after the disaster April 7th 1845. Although Whitefield drew this Hudson River scene and other newsworthy items while a "correspondent for the Illustrated London News" in the 1850s, he did essentially little topical illustration. Lithograph, 7½ × 14. *Photo courtesy of The Mariners Museum, Newport News, Va.*

ABOVE: *Exploring Party in Minnesota.* / *Encampment on Fairy Lake July 1857,* the first of four lithographs in Whitefield's series *Minnesota Scenery.* Twenty-five years after Whitefield and his family had abandoned Minnesota, they returned for a visit. Fairy Lake was one of the few sites which retained the names Whitefield had given them. 10 × 14¾. *Courtesy Print Department, Boston Public Library.*

FACING PAGE, LEFT: Original wash drawing for one of the interchangeable scenes on the Mississippi. "Kandotta" on the steamboat probably represented

Whitefield's subtle advertisement of his real estate venture in Minnesota. Pen, pencil, and wash; signed "E. Whitefield," c. 1858. 8½ × 5½. *Private collection.*

FACING PAGE, RIGHT: Advertisement for First Series / *Views on the Upper Mississippi,* with extravagant claims by Whitefield. Only six of the advertised eight scenes are known. 8⅜ × 5½. Probably intended as a jacket for the lithographs. *Courtesy Print Department, Boston Public Library.*

WHITEFIELD'S PATENT
Combination Drawing Cards.

FIRST SERIES,

VIEWS ON THE UPPER MISSISSIPPI.

These Cards can be used seperately, in the same manner as any other Drawing Cards; but their distinguishing peculiarity consists in this: That by a novel and peculiar arrangement, any two or more of them will unite perfectly to form a picture.

Each series contains eight Cards, and these are capable of being so combined as to form

FIFTY THOUSAND DIFFERENT PICTURES!

No two of which will be alike.

In cases where two sets will combine, 22,277,446,224,310 different pictures can be formed, so that if a person had commenced arranging them at the Creation of the World, and continued his work through sleepless days and nights, at the rate of one combination a minute, he would not yet have completed more than the TEN THOUSANDTH PART OF HIS TASK !

THESE ARE ALL NEW VIEWS, TAKEN EXPRESSLY FOR THIS WORK.

These Cards will also form a very pleasing amusement for a Winter's evening. Any person, too, can have a frame fitted to hold three of them, and every week show his friends a new picture. Various other applications, which will occur to the ingenious, can be made of this novelty.   Other series are in preparation ; among them will be—

2d.   HUDSON RIVER SCENERY.
3d.   EUROPEAN VIEWS.
4th. LAKES OF MINNESOTA.

Retail Price, 50 Cents Each Series.

Published by E. WHITEFIELD, 52 LaSalle St., Chicago.

☞ A PATENT APPLIED FOR—⚐

NEAR BROWNSVILLE. MINN.

BLUFF BELOW LANSING. IOWA.

Near Brownsville, Minn., Bluff below Lansing, Iowa, From Davenport, Iowa, and Approach to Winona, Minn., four of the Combination Drawing Cards published in 1858. Tinted lithographs, each 8½ × 5½. Photo courtesy Chicago Historical Society.

FROM DAVENPORT, IOWA

APPROACH TO WINONA, MINN.

Republican Wigwam./Site of the Republican Convention in Chicago which nominated Abraham Lincoln for President in 1860. The candidacy of Lincoln is the only one known for which Whitefield published lithographs. 6¾ × 11. *Private collection.*

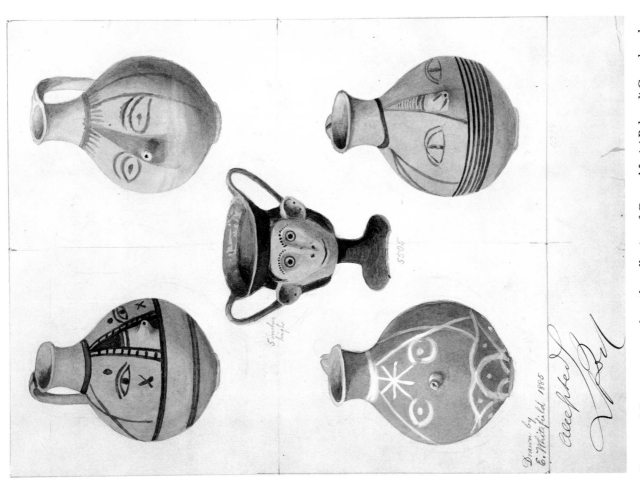

Drawn by
E. Whitefield 1885

Accepted

Drawing of Cypriote pottery from the collection of General Luigi Palma di Cesnola, whose signature of approval of the rendering is in the lower left corner. Signed watercolor on bristol board, 14 × 10. *Private collection.*

illustrations of Colonial houses—were ideas which Whitefield proposed and saw to fruition.

Throughout his life, landscape, especially a body of water, was a constant subject matter. Perhaps most typical of his unwavering interest are the many sketches whose titles begin "looking up-," "looking down-," or "approach to,"—quick renderings done from the deck of a steamboat. One sketchbook of houses for *Homes of our Forefathers* in the collection of the Society for the Preservation of New England Antiquities contains eleven wash drawings of Spot Pond, conceivably within walking distance of Whitefield's home of fifteen years in Reading, Massachusetts.

The twenty-five sketchbooks at the Society and at the Boston Public Library give an extensive graphic account of Colonial New England houses. There is no evidence that Whitefield intended these drawings for anything but lithographs, that is, thought of the sketches as marketable. Indeed, one of the most delightful sketchbooks is full of very pleasingly rendered wash drawings: the Lynde house, Melrose; Poor house, Newbury; Palmer in Salem; Old Meeting House in Hingham; Iron Works in Saugus; Pillsbury in Newburyport; Craddock in Medford; Alden in Duxbury, and many more equally as important. It says on the cover: "Old Sketches of no use—They are on good Drawing Paper, & the *backs* can be used again."

II

On August 1, 1842, Whitefield wrote: "I also at length, accomplished that which I have so long desired, namely, I obtained everything necessary to commence *Oil Painting.* For three years have I been longing to obtain them, but could not afford to do so. What success I shall meet with remains to be seen."

His caution was well-advised. Of those oils which have been seen, most are less interesting, less well painted, than his other work. But the two views of Montreal are delightful. A much later oil, a view of Lake

Winnepesaukee, is also charming. Well-painted, sunny pictures, with charming jewellike color and clear detail, they are a delight to look at. Carefully worked, they are vivid examples of Whitefield's catholic interest in landscape, botany, and architecture.

There probably exist other oils of city views or prominent landscapes than those referred to in the diaries, or in known collections. The location of many is unknown. The $200 commission for the view of St. Peter's may have been one. Many were undoubtedly shown at the Toronto Exhibition. A guess at those viewed by Canadians in 1856 would include the views of Montreal and Hamilton, and Tadoussac; also scenes of the great Canadian Falls—of the Ottawa, La Puce, the Chaudiere, the St. Anne, the Montmorenci. Two oils of Canadian Falls are owned by the Boston Public Library, though most of the Canadian subjects whose location is known are owned by our northern neighbors. It is hoped that more will surface, of the quality of the views of Montreal.

III

The diaries and other papers in the Whitefield collection at the Boston Public Library have made it possible to collate a list of the city views and clarify the manner in which they were executed. Three of those on Stokes' list in *American Historical Prints, Early Views of American Cities, &c.,* belong to Whitefield's earlier *North American Scenery* series. The last part of the title for the large folio views, *Whitefield's Original Views of American Cities,* was informally changed to *North American Views of American Cities* when Whitefield went to work in Canada, and, still later, to *North American Scenery* to accommodate Niagara Falls.

Publication of views was dependent on acquiring an adequate number of subscribers. The diaries show constant communication with his publishers and agents. Mentioned were Groves in Canada; Holmes, Foss, and Palmatary in Pennsylvania; and Benjamin, Francis, and George Smith, who traveled widely in Ohio, New York, Connecticut, Rhode Island, and even St. John's, New Brunswick. A letter in 1849 from Benjamin Smith, from Salem, Massachusetts, suggested that Whitefield could sell a print of Danvers, if it were a good one, and the view of Lynn should be fairly large. But Whitefield was his own best salesman. Armed with lists of a town's most notable citizens, whom he saw in order of their importance, he solicited signatures for his subscription books. At Port Hope, Canada, late in 1855, he "Called around among the folks and the Mayor assured me that he would make up the number I lack." (The Council bailed out the Mayor ten days later, when they subscribed for two sets.) Often, when Whitefield returned with the finished lithograph, he would ask for a signed statement which he would

From Nature by E. Whitefield

Looking up Lake Pepin./Views on the Mississippi, No 5. Most typical, perhaps, of Whitefield's career, spent on the decks of steamboats going up and down the Mississippi, Hudson, Saint Lawrence, and countless smaller rivers of the northern United States and Canada. Wash drawing, signed. 7½ × 12. *Photo courtesy Minnesota Historical Society.*

publish later in circulars advertising his work. The lengthy *Opinions of the Press*, published in 1854, listed thirty-eight favorable press notices on fifteen views, and "A vast number of notices similar to these could be added were there room sufficient for the purpose."

Discouraged at times, he found that solicitation was "getting to be dull work" and "the stragglers are not worth it." At one time he noted that he was "running around all day collecting, but with poor success as almost everybody is at the Toronto celebration for the opening of the Hamilton & Toronto RR." Some subscribers, overcome by Whitefield's persuasiveness and the impressive circulars, probably found themselves unable to pay when Whitefield returned to collect. Back in London, Canada West, in 1856, he "made arrangements with a man to sue my non-paying subscribers." Even in the midst of his Minnesota adventure, he "Went to St. Anthony this morning and was engaged all day in trying law-suits for my views." One sketchbook at the Society for the Preservation of New England Antiquities has several short but loaded sentences:

Old subs. who did not subscribe the second time, nor to me. [4 names]
Persons who paid Smith. [3 names]
Good Witnesses. [4 names]

Whitefield even brought legal action against one of his agents, Foss, in Philadelphia, in 1850:

Commenced delivering the Views this morng and the men soon returned saying that Foss had promised them for $3, or colored, or a dozen other stupid things. . . . this is most outrageous—what course shall I pursue. I am for putting them down at once at $3 but Tompkins will not hear of it.

[That November] Found Foss had been doing the business for me so got out a warrant for his arrest, but did not catch him. . . . Met the Constable at 7 A.M, and routed up Mr. Foss—took him before the alderman when he agreed to settle at once—did so on condition that he would pay me the money he had collected & give a receipt in full of all accounts—Paid part of it—Spent the rest of the day collecting—Poor luck.

Whitefield's relations with his other agents were not entirely trouble-free. He was periodically disappointed with the efforts of one or another of them, like Groves, in Canada. After Whitefield conferred with him and discovered how little he had done, the artist called on the editors himself. He seems to have judged Groves harshly in this case, however:

The people here think that it is impossible to obtain a good view of their place on account of its being situated on such level ground, and it requires some talking to overcome their prejudice on this point.

Francis Smith had been working as an agent for Whitefield since

Hubbard House, Concord, Massachusetts, from the sketchbook labeled by Whitefield, "Old Sketches of No Use. They are on good Drawing Paper, and the *Backs* can be used again." Numerous notes on the sketches reminded Whitefield of colors, changes in depiction, people to see, relevant historical facts. "Probably built about 1670" and torn down around 1872. Pencil and wash, 4½ × 7. *Photo courtesy Society for the Preservation of New England Antiquities.*

1846, in Cincinnati, Rochester, and Wheeling, among other places. He and George were responsible for more than 1200 subscribers to the Providence views. There are references to problems with Smith in 1850, and the isolated sentences quoted above, but Whitefield evidently trusted him enough that year that he "gave Smith part of the subscription book for George to use."[16] On an extended trip to Canada in April, 1852, Whitefield arrived in Montreal, walking across half the harbor on ice, and canoeing the rest of the way.

This was about 6 P.M. . . . I saw the editors and quite a number of the subscribers before night, and the View takes very well indeed. Not a trace can I find of Smith or any of his crew, so that there is little doubt but that all will go well here. At all events he cannot hurt me much now.

[On another trip in July] Who should make his appearance here but master F. Smith, who wished to sell me out his subscription books of Montreal & Quebec, I accordingly paid him $50 for them. I cannot well make less than $50 by the operation, and at the same time keep him from meddling with me in these two places.

Francis Smith is never again mentioned in the diaries.

The Smith Brothers, publishers, were actively producing city views, most drawn by J. W. Hill, trailing Whitefield by four to ten years with views of Brooklyn; Salem, Massachusetts; Portsmouth, New Hampshire; Albany, New York; Portland, Maine; and Boston. Several drawn by Whitefield were published in conjunction with the Smiths, namely, *Boston in 1848*, *Portland, Me.* (1848), and the two views of Providence, R.I. in 1849. A Smith view of Oswego, New York, was put on stone by D. W. Moody,[17] undoubtedly the same Moody Whitefield employed to help with the Cincinnati and Brooklyn views, and who lithographed several plates for Dr. Strong's *American Flora*. By the time of the publication of *Hartford* and *Worcester*, Whitefield and the Smiths were no longer working together.

The diaries hint at a consequence, if not a reason. On May 17,

1855, Whitefield, who was in Toronto, received a telegram from New York saying that the Fern trial was due to come up in court at any moment. Whitefield promptly left, and waited in New York for five days for the trial to commence. On May 30, an edgy Whitefield returned to Canada to continue collecting, and on June 5 left again for New York, arriving just as the trial began. Fern had brought a suit of libel against Francis and G. Warren Smith. While working as an agent for the Smith Brothers, and collecting for a view of Brooklyn,[18] Fern had sent a letter to the subscribers stating that his employers were planning to produce a view inferior to the one they proposed, and that he planned to publish a better one. The Smith Brothers had then counterattacked with their own letter to the subscribers and an acrid rebuttal published in the Brooklyn papers. Fearful of the outcome of the trial, Whitefield hired another lawyer and found new witnesses for Fern, with whom his sympathies lay. Fern lost the suit, and was ordered to pay court costs of $484.14.[19]

Whitefield's name does not appear on the list of witnesses, since they were recorded for the purpose of assessing Fern, but it is to be assumed that Whitefield was a witness for the former Smith agent. It is a temptation to surmise that Whitefield hoped for vicarious gratification for injuries he felt he had suffered from Francis Smith five years earlier. The Smith Brothers indeed did not publish views of Montreal or Quebec in this period. Perhaps the Smiths were involved in Whitefield's misadventure with the publication of his views of New York. At any event, Whitefield was interested enough in the trial to make two trips from Toronto to New York, at the loss of both time and money—and this for a man who was compulsive about not wasting time. He once sketched Harper's Ferry during a lay-over in port: "instead of eating dinner as most of the passengers did, I spent the precious minutes (20) and seeing all I could see, and in sketching all I could sketch."

Although Whitefield had help drawing the views of Brooklyn and

Cincinnati on stone, as a rule from the time of the publication of the view of Newburgh, New York, in 1846, he executed and oversaw the production of most of them himself. He touched up improperly colored prints, and changed lithographers if he was not satisfied: "Went to New York and got the stone which I took to a printer of the name of Newman, as I am tired of Michelin." (It was 1848 and probably the same Newman who, with Jones, printed the *North American Scenery* series.) Twenty-five copies of the views of Toronto delivered to the City Council were colored by the Whitefield sons.[20] Whitefield made many trips to the lithographers, to "touch up my views," or draw tints.

The prices for views varied from $1.50 for a view of Chicago, sold through the Art Union of that city, and $2 for a view of Paris, Canada West, to a view of Brantford, colored, for $15. The views of Philadelphia, due to the carelessness of the agent, Foss, were almost sold for only $3. The Public Library of Galena, Illinois, owns a testy letter to the Galena town fathers. Whitefield complained of not being paid in full for his view of that city, and suggested that they either give him more money, or buy more views. The special committee of the town fathers, with equal rancor, denied Whitefield's assertion and pointed out that the views for which he wanted $8 were being sold around town for $4.

The following manuscript contract is in the Boston Public Library:

Toronto, Feb. 2, 1854

This agreement is made between Edwin Whitefield on the one part and Messrs Maclear & Co. of the City of Toronto on the other part; That is to say, We, Maclear & Co. agree to deliver to the order of E. Whitefield at our store all the views of the City of Toronto or other cities of Canada which may be left in our care, free of charge; but should we have to make collections for the said E. Whitefield we will charge ten per cent on all monies collected by us. Also all new subscribers which we may obtain for any of the views of the Cities of Canada as published by Mr E. Whitefield we shall charge twenty-five per cent. Mr. Whitefield hereby agreeing to allow us the above rates for collecting and obtaining new subscribers, and we agreeing to use all diligence in the collection of debts, &c.

E. Whitefield
Maclear & Co.

It is understood that the following will be the prices charged on my views.

One view .... Five Dollars
Two Do .... Eight "
Three .... Eleven "
Four .... Twelve "
Five .... Fifteen "

These views are the following:

1 Quebec
1 Montreal
1 Toronto
1 Hamilton
1 London

It is also understood that the above prices are for *tinted views*; and that no deduction will be made, nor commission allowed on the extra price (Three dollars per copy) for colored views.

On the above commutation prices also from Ten to Twenty per cent will be allowed according as the number of copies subscribed for may be more or less.

E. Whitefield

The diary page of Tuesday, June 19, 1866, illustrates the financial arrangements between artist and lithographer (see page 48).

The preliminary sketches for the city views are marvels of delicate pencil work—an accurate delineation with hair-thin lines. The surviving examples are therefore less common than the pen and wash drawings; their fragile rendering has been almost rubbed away in many cases. Most important is the sketchbook bought by the New York Public Library in late 1973. It spans 1846-1863, and contains many sketches for the New York view, a trip along the Ohio River, and towns in Michigan, among others. Among the best preserved are two sketchbooks for his last city view, *Quincy, Mass.* Various notebooks and subscription books have steeples and facades interspersed among his writings.

Whitefield's views were faithful representations of careful observation. He depicted distance simply and skillfully, and became more at ease with the complex perspective in successive views. In some sketchbooks, notably that of Hamilton, Canada West, in the Public Archives of Canada, there are whole streets sketched in four or five diagonal layers across a page. A comparison with the finished view finds them all in the same scale, and in the proper perspective. The steps from these sketches to the drawing on stone involved more than is depicted by the rudimentary numbering system on each page. He probably correlated the sketches with a mapping system, drawn from his walking tours. As early as 1846 he was working on a map of "West Chester." Part of the answer may lie with the drawing of Troy, New York, owned by the Gardiners. It consists of three pages of transparent paper glued together, measuring 8⅞ inches by 39 inches, which was probably used to transfer the drawing to the stone. Although the print has not yet been located, there is reference to it on Stokes' list, with the measurements 39.8 x 22.8. The width would tally, and there would be 14″ in the height left for foreground and sky.

The first view published by Whitefield—Albany, New York—is a charming vista framed by trees. Although Albany is quite detailed, it is in the background of a rural scene. The landscape is very quickly subordinated to the city in subsequent views; in many of the ones that followed, prominent in the foreground is a characteristic young tree that resembles a newly-planted maple. Whitefield's time outdoors was spent accurately portraying the topography and the architecture; later, indoors, the foreground was applied. In many cases it was probably not part of the scene till drawn on stone. *Troy*, the first view put on stone by Whitefield, presented no problems; the foreground consisted of storage docks. *Newburgh* has four single trees in the foreground plane, like an altar screen.

The part of the view of Brooklyn probably done by Moody is clarified by comparison with the preliminary watercolor in the New-York Historical Society, which is of Brooklyn only, with no foreground. However, there is enough variety in the level of skill in the execution of the foreground and a comparison with other lithographs drawn only by Moody to suggest that Whitefield drew the middle part, with the U.S. Hotel and the Ferry, and the work to either side was done by Moody, an inferior draftsman.

The view of Buffalo is absolutely flat; Whitefield found it an uninteresting city, for which he compensated by drawing in fourteen named steamboats and three schooners. *Newark* and *Portland* are similar; Whitefield had not yet mastered a foreground scene that did not look like a scattering of trees.

An interesting fact emerged from the collection at the Essex Institute in Salem, Massachusetts. They have four copies of the view of Salem, but the first three are of a previously little-known lithograph published by "F. Michlin" in 1849, one year before the well-known view of *Salem, Lynn, Beverly, and Danvers, Mass.*, published by Endicott. The latter was taken from the former, but the foreground was changed. It is decidedly inferior to the Michlin print, which has very delicate crayon work, many charming details such as the train crossing the harbor, and generally more careful and pleasing rendering. The lines of the Endicott version are even and mechanical. From 1850, generally the better views are those which Whitefield drew on the stone himself.

The first three views executed after Endicott became publisher consist of multiple scenes on one stone: *Panoramic Views of Philadelphia; Salem, Lynn, Beverly, and Danvers, Mass.*; and *View of Trenton, N.J.* Evidently, the views of New York, which were to be three views of the city, were slated for publication by Endicott also.

The view of Trenton was one of Whitefield's most ambitious prints. There is a center view, approximately 21″ x 34″; a top view, 4″ x 9″; and five views along the bottom, one at 3″ x 3″, one at 3″ x 6″ and three at 6″ x 3″ (measurements approximate). Twenty-seven locations are identified in script below the main view.

By the time of the publication of *Poughkeepsie*, Whitefield's handling of the foreground was fully developed, and, with its topographically attractive horizon with College Hill, its varying tones, and its skillful drawing, it is one of the most attractive. Others produced at this time equally well-handled are those of *Montreal, Quebec, and Toronto*; the latter was successful because Whitefield drew it at an oblique angle, with the waterfront and cross streets running at diagonals. It is also very detailed and accurate. In fact, Whitefield was able to quote in his *Opinions of the Press*, "I am glad to say that Mr. White-

Page from a sketchbook showing steeples of churches in New York City, one of the working drawings for the ill-fated view. Pencil, 3⅝ × 5⅞. *Courtesy Print Department, Boston Public Library.*

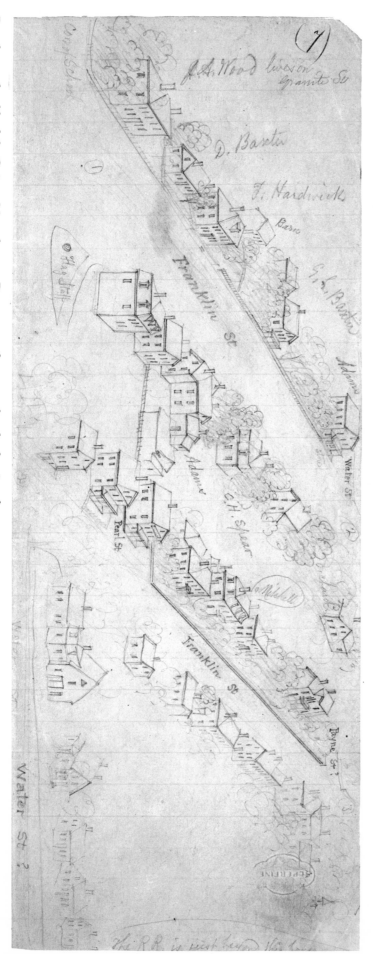

Page from a sketchbook for Quincy, Massachusetts. Done twenty-five years after the drawings for the New York view, this sketchbook illustrates well Whitefield's unabated skill and accuracy with the pencil. 2¾ × 5½. Private collection.

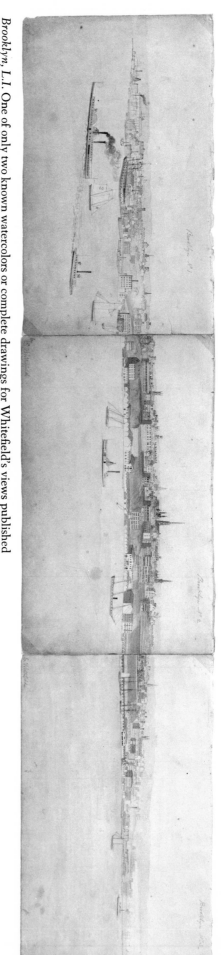

Brooklyn, L.I. One of only two known watercolors or complete drawings for Whitefield's views published between 1845 and 1857. 8¼ × 40. Courtesy of the Print Room, New-York Historical Society.

Detail of *Salem, Mass.*, lithograph drawn on stone by Whitefield and printed by Michelin, New York, in 1849. *Courtesy Essex Institute.*

field has achieved a great feat—he has drawn a good view of Toronto; a thing scarcely deemed possible.—Anglo-American Magazine."

Many misconceptions exist about a Whitefield view of New York. Stokes, in his listing in *American Historical Prints, Early Views of American Cities, &c.*, mentions that the *stone* broke upon the first impression. There is a scrap of paper in the Whitefield collection at the Boston Public Library that says, in most probably the hand of his wife, Lillian, "*Steel plate* of View of New York was burnt up 1851 Philadelphia fire"; the Stokes Supplementary List of Prints in *Iconography of Manhattan* mentions views which fit the description of the Whitefield views, as possibly by Robert Havell.[21] Both the New-York Historical Society and the Royal Ontario Museum, Sigmund Samuel Collection, own impressions of New York views, signed E. Whitefield. There is no lettering on any.

One would assume that a print of New York would be very important for an artist making his primary livelihood from the sale of his city views. One would also assume that no artist who sketched almost all the major cities east of the Mississippi would ignore New York; although many views had been produced by many lithographers, in a vast and rapidly growing city there was always room for one more. And there are at least five pages of sketches of New York in the Whitefield sketchbook at the New York Public Library. Stokes was aware that there had been a mishap with the Whitefield view. Entries in Whitefield's diary for 1850, when he was running constantly between New York, Philadelphia, and Trenton, coupled with an analysis of other known work of the artist in question, leads to the conclusion that Whitefield's views were engraved by Robert Hinshelwood.[22]

What happened in the production? Whitefield was indeed in Philadelphia during a big fire (in 1850, however), but he mentions no personal loss, and one would wonder why he had the plate there. He does mention Butler, an engraver, with whom he "had a long talk" shortly *before* the fire, and, upon his return to New York on the day following it, he sought out Hinshelwood. There is no mention in the

diaries for solicitation for a view of New York; it is possible that the missing diary for 1851 would link the story of the New York view with the story of the rupture with the Smith Brothers. Perhaps Whitefield had an agreement with them to produce a steel engraving, and, after the mishap, whatever it was, the publishers opted for forgetting the whole production. This might explain Whitefield's feeling that he had been hurt by them, and his subsequent interest in the Fern trial. For a man who was so taciturn, possibly unconcerned, with social encounters with friends or fellow artists, this seems a feasible explanation.

The *Providence* views, *North* and *South*, published in 1849, were incorrectly printed. The same letter stone, reading *From the South*, was used for both. (The view showing the two artificial lagoons is, correctly, *From the North;* the one of a jetty and the waterfront, *From the South.*) Most prints were corrected after printing in almost undetectable pencil work; the letters involved were erased and changed. On one print the lettering was either corrected on the stone or a pen was used very successfully to simulate a lithograph line. One set of views, at the American Antiquarian Society, has extensive penciling on the image, most of the view *From the South;* windows and occasional doors on many foreground buildings have been added, as is the name *Perry* on the side of a steamboat. In the sketchbook acquired in 1972 from the Old Print Shop by the New York Public Library, there are sketches for the views, including a full-page drawing of the *Perry.* These views (as well as Whitefield's view of Boston) were put on stone by C. W. Burton, a very competent lithographic artist, and were well done.[23] It is even possible that Whitefield's obvious dissatisfaction with the detail, and the incorrect title, contributed to his anger towards the Smiths.

The series of seven views of Chicago which Whitefield drew between 1860 and 1863 combine an accurate record of that city prior to the Great Fire on October 8, 1871, with historical reference to Lincoln campaigns. John Drury wrote in *The Magazine Antiques* that both Douglas and Lincoln, on successive nights, addressed the people of Chicago from the balcony of the Tremont House in the senatorial campaign of 1858, and Lincoln used it as his headquarters in the 1860 presidential campaign. Other areas of the city depicted are the Illinois and Michigan Central Railroad Depot, the bridges over the canal, the Sherman House and Court House. The view of the Rush St. Bridge shows the McCormick Reaper factory. The view of Michigan Ave. and Michigan Terrace shows another view of the Illinois and Michigan Central Depot; the tower of the near church is probably where Whitefield sat to sketch the first view. The Chicago Historical Society

has a photograph of the Illinois and Michigan Central Depot, taken by A. Halsey in 1858, the same scene as one of Whitefield's Chicago series. While the lithograph is larger, Whitefield may have used the photograph as the basis for the view; he had used, with acknowledgment, a daguerreotype for the Lynn portion of *Salem, Lynn, Beverly, and Danvers, Mass.,* executed in 1850. Whitefield may simply have sat in the same spot as the photographer. If he did use the photograph for the basis of the lithograph, he omitted and elaborated as he saw fit, enlivening the scene by adding a few small sail boats and row boats in the canal, and a topsail schooner tied up at dock.

The view of the Tremont House gave Whitefield a great deal of trouble. On July 8, 1861, he pronounced it not good, and subsequently the stone cracked on the first impression. The new one was ready in August.

The series which Whitefield executed after he arrived in Massachusetts to live, with the exception of the first two, *View of the Public Garden & Boston Common,* and *Fitchburg, Mass.,* are different from the earlier city views. There is no stage-setting foreground, less attention to the tiny portrayal of an active city, and a generally more abbreviated rendering. The legacy of these later views is the original wash drawings and watercolors. There are seven:

View of the Public Garden & Boston Common, two versions, at the Boston Athenæum and the Museum of Fine Arts, Boston.
View of Fitchburg, Mass., at the Fitchburg Art Museum.
View of Portsmouth, N.H., at the Museum of Fine Arts, Boston.
Malden, Mass., also at the Museum of Fine Arts, Boston.
View of Dedham, Mass., at the Dedham Historical Society.
View of Worcester, Mass., at the Worcester Art Museum.
View of Lowell, Mass., at the Canadiana Collection, Royal Ontario Museum, Toronto, Canada.

A lovely watercolor of Boston, Massachusetts, on four sketchbook pages was evidently never put on stone. Probably Whitefield intended to do a second, later version, as he had with Worcester.

Portsmouth, New Hampshire. Original wash drawing for the view from Mount Vernon Street looking across the South Mill-Pond. Pencil and wash, 15½ × 30¼. Courtesy M. and M. Karolik Collection, Museum of Fine Arts, Boston.

Both views of Portsmouth, done in 1873, and the views of Amesbury, Worcester, Lowell, Malden, and Newburyport, done in 1876, were reproduced as sepia photographs. Whitefield himself regarded this method with displeasure; one half of one of the views of Portsmouth was used as the backing for a Whitefield watercolor (owned by Essex Institute, Salem, Mass.). A print of *Newburyport, Mass.*, at the Boston Athenæum, has the church spires and distant horizon drawn in, in Whitefield's unmistakable hand.

The preliminary watercolors and pencil drawings do not show an abbreviated, mechanical, short-cut production. They are conceived in the same manner as his earlier efforts, with delicate pencil work, great detail on the more architecturally interesting buildings, soft washes.

City views offered, at an inexpensive price to an increasing middle-class clientele, a pictorial representation of their own towns. Other topographical artists prominent at the time, besides Whitefield and J. W. Hill, were W. J. Bennett, Robert Havell, William H. Bartlett, and August Kollner. All but Hill and Kollner were from England, and Hill was the son of the English artist, J. Hill, who had emigrated to the United States at the beginning of the century.

Lithography came to life in this country at the moment of the birth of industry; the Erie and Ohio Canals inaugurated a national transportation system admirably supported by steamboat navigation at the precise time of the desire to expand westward. This was an incredibly fortunate juxtaposition of events in a country spilling over with en-

53

thusiasm and new nationalism. The desire to record and disseminate accounted for the fevered production of views of cities and national scenery. Whitefield, like dozens of artists, lithographers, and publishers, took advantage of the mood of the country.

IV

The blessing which belongs to those who revere old landmarks and seek to preserve memorials of the past should rest with Mr. Whitefield.... The views are drawn by Mr. Whitefield with scrupulous fidelity, and they constitute a study over which one who is interested in old New England life might linger delightedly for hours.[24]

Courtesy Print Department, Boston Public Library.

By the time this assessment of Whitefield was written in the Boston *Journal*, he had published three volumes of *Homes of our Forefathers*; the first, *Homes . . . in Massachusetts*, had been published in three editions. While drawing the views of towns in Massachusetts, he had

begun collecting sketches and wash drawings from nature of many of the old New England houses. He appreciated landscape and terrain with an observant and sensitive eye, and was impressed with one of the great characteristics of the Colonial house—its most satisfactory siting. Admiration for the scale, material, and gentle aging are all portrayed in the many pencil sketches, wash drawings, and watercolors which he executed for the books.

Whitefield talked with old residents, visited town halls, and sought out deeds in the county registries throughout New England for verification of dates and names. Abbott Lowell Cummings, director of the Society for the Preservation of New England Antiquities, has pointed out that a date assigned by Whitefield to the Boardman house in Saugus (1686/7), although almost fifty years later than the one commonly believed, is the correct one. A booklet at the Society has produced Whitefield's rough draft for a letter:

Newport

I have for many years been engaged in sketching the historical houses of New England and collecting whatever facts there may be of interest connected with them. I shall be highly gratified if you can grant me a brief interview at an hour that may be convenient to yourself as I should like to ask you a few questions, especially in reference to your birth-place. I am stopping at 27 High St. where an answer to this communication will reach me.

In conclusion, I beg to subscribe myself,

Very Respectfully Yours

Both the Boston Public Library and the Society for the Preservation of New England Antiquities own many letters from owners of houses; the latter has the following example:

I return your sketch, with some changes in the L part.... You have got the lower windows in the end of the house as they should be. Neither of them should appear as a door.... The two chimnies on the main house

From Nature by E. Whitefield

"Beard Orchard" in Reading, Massachusetts, Whitefield's home for eighteen years. The house, just off Main Street, is no longer standing. From here, Whitefield worked on all but the last two volumes of *Homes of our Forefathers*. Although he coyly penciled in "residence of E. Whitefield" on one small photoreproduction, he did not include it in the illustrations. Signed pencil-and-wash drawing, 5½ × 7. *Photo courtesy of the Boston Public Library*.

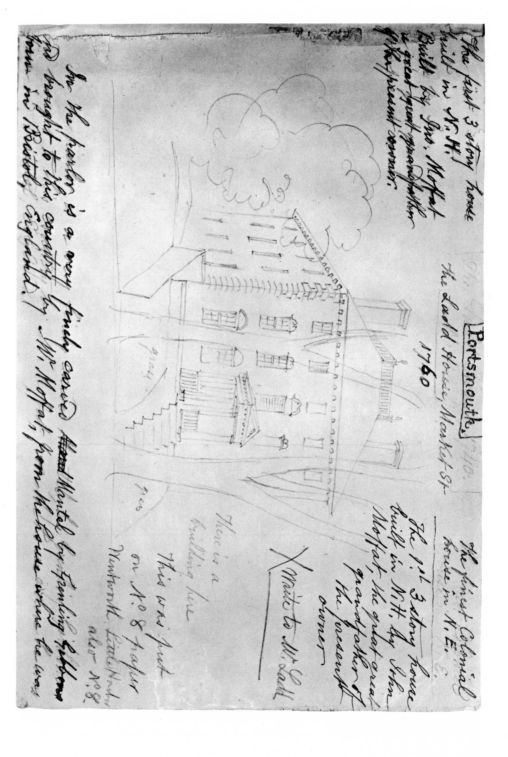

The Moffatt-Ladd House, Portsmouth, New Hampshire. With fast, sure lines, Whitefield captured the flavor of a house, adding factual details and information later. This is the one illustration in all the books of the series *The Homes of our Forefathers* which appears as a photograph; possibly Whitefield could not complete, or lost, the finished drawing; but felt the house too important not to include in the volume devoted to houses in Maine, New Hampshire, and Vermont. Pencil sketch, 5¾ × 8½. Photo courtesy Society for the Preservation of New England Antiquities.

have square caps over them, supported by bricks at the corners. . . . I believe this answers all your questions; but I am so interested in your getting everything as it should be, that I hope you will ask further questions, if you have doubts how anything should be represented.

Chs. H. Bell

1 March, 1886

Mr. Bell sent another letter:

There is no door on the side of the L, although there was one when the photograph was taken. It is better not to put it in, as it did not belong to the original building.

This letter shows one of Whitefield's routes to accuracy, but it also suggests that he occasionally worked from photographs. This was not general practice, however, as his letter of introduction indicates. In many sketchbooks for the houses, there are also wash drawings of landscapes through which he traveled: "Piscataqua River / Schooner is going up Cochico R. to Dover" (the Maine–New Hampshire border); sketches of "The Common–South Royalston" and "Bennington, a branch of the Walloomac" (Vermont). There is one photograph reproduced in the Homes . . . in Maine, New Hampshire, and Vermont, published in 1886.

Whitefield made very quick rough sketches in pencil. To some he added details with pen, to some, wash, and to others, both. Occasionally the pen work was done with a thin watercolor line, sometimes red, as in the pleasing one of Drowne House, Barrington, Rhode Island. The pen would delineate the roof lines, the window panes, the doors; the more dramatic of his efforts have darkened panes. The rapidly executed line was always thin, delicate, and spidery, but not nervous, and the effect is of antiquity at rest.

The finished drawings, ready for transfer to stone, are clearly and accurately drawn; often, blue lines heighten the important lines. Examples in the Boston Public Library collection are the Gray House, used as a British hospital after the Battle of Bunker Hill; the Tremere

House, dating from 1674; the Hancock Tavern, Corn Court, dating from 1634; Green Dragon Tavern, a meeting-place during the Revolution but razed in 1828; and the Waldo House, where the British Major Pitcairn died. All the streets in the North End are still there, populated before the start of the twentieth century with Italian immigrants and their descendants. Almost none of the houses remain. Since most of the models fell to the early twentieth-century tenement development, the drawings and lithographs are a valuable record— although not suitable for restoration reference, yet more accurate than many picturesque etchings.

Homes of our Forefathers in Boston, Old England, and Boston, New England contains many of these historic Boston buildings. The Boston Journal commented, on December 19, 1889,

The Wells Mansion, which once stood in the North End of Boston, Massachusetts. This drawing was ready for transfer to the lithographic stone. Whitefield printed from large stones with as many as forty illustrations on each. Pencil, heightened with blue pencil. 3⅛ × 4¾. Courtesy Print Department, Boston Public Library.

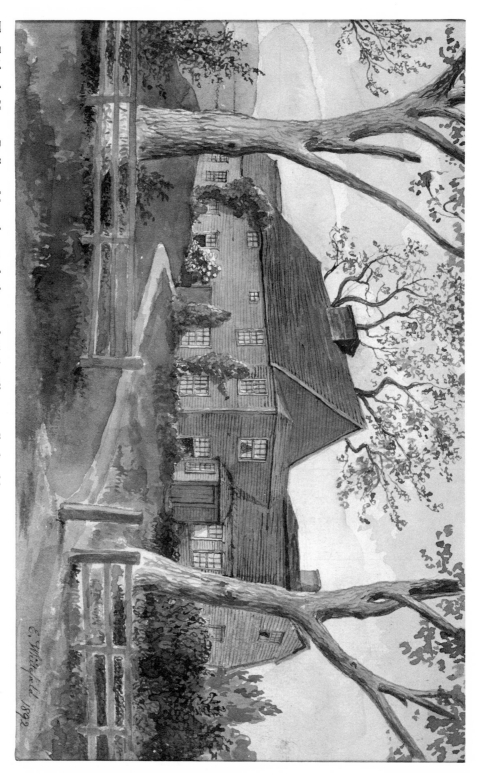

The Fairbanks House, Dedham, Massachusetts, built around 1636, still reportedly the oldest frame house in New England. Watercolor, 5½ × 8⅞. *Private collection.*

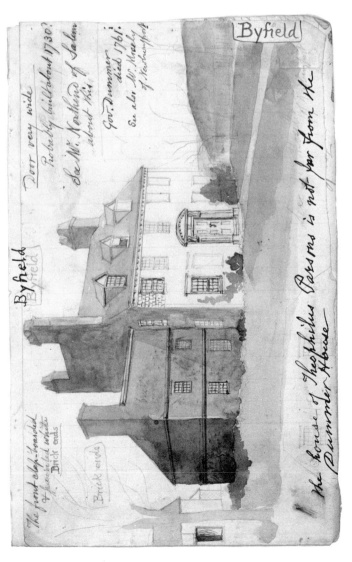

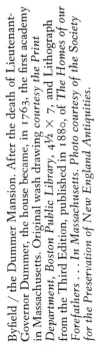

Byfield
Byfield

Door very wide

Probably built about 1730?

See Mr. Northend of Salem about this

Gov. Dummer died 1761.

See also W. Mosely of Newburyport

The front slop-hipped & hipped at the Brick ends

Brick ends

The house of Theophilus Parsons is not far from the Dummer House

Byfield / the Dummer Mansion. After the death of Lieutenant-Governor Dummer, the house became, in 1763, the first academy in Massachusetts. Original wash drawing *courtesy the Print Department, Boston Public Library, 4½ × 7,* and Lithograph from the Third Edition, published in 1880, of *The Homes of our Forefathers . . . In Massachusetts. Photo courtesy of the Society for the Preservation of New England Antiquities.*

There are in all forty pictures of noteworthy old Boston buildings—houses, taverns, and churches. Some of them stand in places where their antiquity is unsuspected and their history unknown. The interest of some of the places is enhanced by the fact that even since Mr. Whitefield began his work they have been pulled down to give place to more modern structures. . . . we cannot easily exaggerate the service which Mr. Whitefield has rendered in preserving them. . . .

The preface to Volume I, *Homes . . . in Massachusetts*, states that

The object of this book is to preserve and hand down to all future posterity representations of the *Homes of Their Forefathers*. From a variety of causes they are rapidly disappearing; and before long the places that now know them will know them no more. It has been a labor of love to the undersigned to collect these mementoes of the past, and his efforts have been ably seconded by many gentlemen to whom his thanks are hereby returned. . . . He has tried to do his work faithfully, and no liberties have been taken with the old buildings represented, or with their surroundings, merely for pictorial effect.

The foreword to the New Edition in 1892, "To Those Who Are Interested in the Early History of New England," is basically the same, with the addition,

Of these [800 sketches] he has published, in the five volumes thus far issued, about one-half that number, at a heavy expense to himself, without the least assistance from any person except what he has derived from the sale of these books, which have so far not equalled the outlays of one kind or another by upwards of nine thousand dollars. . . . This statement is made not by way of complaint but simply because it is a fact; and that the present and future generations may know under what circumstances this collection has been gathered together. . . .

Both the wash drawings and the pen and pencil sketches are more charming than the finished lithographs. But the latter deserve more credit than was given them by Colonel Henry Lee, who showed the Massachusetts Historical Society copies of Whitefield's *Homes of our Forefathers* and a book of etchings of old buildings in Boston by

Tolman, "and remarked that both these books possessed considerable interest and value, and the latter had also some artistic merit."[25]

Whitefield's comments in the foreword, edging on the ill-tempered, and the Colonel's evaluation, are facets of the same problem. As documents of the past, the books are valid. As the impetus to historic preservation, they were unquestionably highly important. As wash drawings, they are colorful and engaging. But as lithographs they are relatively lifeless. This is not so with the first volumes, on Massachusetts towns, but very much the case with the more commercial production of the volume devoted to Maine, New Hampshire, and Vermont, which forsook the Gothic lettering on stone for block letterpress, and a more picturesque rendering for a quicker, more abbreviated one. A great deal of the problem is with the tint-stones, which are drab.

More attention was devoted to the Massachusetts volumes. There were three editions, the 1879 subscriber's copy, 1879 (evidently the second edition), and the 1880 third edition. All the lettering was done on the stone. Above each picture, in Gothic letters, appears the name of the town in which the house was situated. Below is the name of the house, and a short description. Forty-three views are common to the first two editions. The 1880 edition is not consistent; the copy in the Houghton Library at Harvard University, Cambridge, Massachusetts, contains six pages of sixteen pictures, not contained in the copy at the Society for the Preservation of New England Antiquities, and ten in the latter's copy are not in the Houghton version. However, the twenty-three found in all three editions are in the Harvard copy, though in a different order.

Whitefield was tired by the constant strain of supporting a family with the lithographic crayon, dreaming up schemes that would appeal to the public. These books of lithographs and historical research involved a great deal of travel and correspondence, undoubtedly more than he had spent on any other project, yet the results went consistently downhill. He derived great pleasure from sketching. His love of a body of water did not abate during the period in which he was drawing Colonial houses; one sketchbook has eleven wash drawings of Spot Pond in Melrose, Massachusetts, close to his home in Reading.

His spirits were revived by the trip to England and Scotland, the countries of his and Lillian's births, in 1888–1889. The resulting publication, *Homes of our Forefathers in Boston, Old England, and Boston, New England,* in regular and deluxe editions, was again as ambitious as the volumes on Massachusetts. The fancier volume, which he published from his home in Roslindale, Massachusetts, is in brown or red Turkish morocco, with gold tooling and lettering. The chromolithographs are pasted on bristol board, one to a page. The original price was $15. The regular edition was published by Damrell & Upham, Boston, also in 1889, for $6.

A clipping collection in the Whitefield papers contains six favorable reviews, from the *Boston Courier,* the *Boston Journal,* the *Boston Evening Transcript,* the *Christian Register,* and two others. Whitefield received little credit from later architectural historians. Vincent Scully, in *Shingle Style,* published in 1955, allotted one half of one footnote to the comment that architectural renovation is impossible from his drawings. Joseph Everett Chandler wrote of the preservation movement in the 1910's in contrast to the "less satisfactory . . . first awakenings of the 1880's," in *The Colonial House,* 1916. Whitefield himself collected many newsclippings with illustrations by other artists in the 1880's, which he pasted among his sketches, and was also critical:

In Frank Leslie's Popular Monthly May/86 is a ridiculous view of the Woodworth House, well, &c. It states that the house is still standing, &c.... All Wrong.

The fact is that he did publish, in 1879, the first record of Colonial houses, which represented work from the mid-1870's, and, as an unidentified newsclipping predicted, in many cases "it is reasonably certain that within a few years Mr. Whitefield's drawings will be the only memorial left."

A few of the houses depicted by Whitefield are owned by the Society for the Preservation of New England Antiquities, incorporated in 1910, and private corporations set up for particular historic houses, like the Wayside Inn, Sudbury, and the Fairbanks House, Dedham. Although many of the houses are not under institutional control, the interest which Whitefield instigated carried many over the dangers of unconcern into the realm of respected antiquity.

V

The range of Whitefield's work is most fully comprehended from the sketchbooks, which record many other towns besides the formidable list of published views. A sketch of "The James River, above Richmond" (Virginia) seems to indicate the southern extremity of his travels. There are no sketches of towns south of St. Louis on the Mississippi, but Whitefield did go up the Missouri River as far as St. Joseph, a large fur-trading station. In 1860, he went up the Rock River of northern Illinois into Wisconsin. His trip on the Erie Rail Road in the fall of 1853 covered the valleys of the Ramapo, the Delaware, the Susquehanna, as well as smaller tributaries: the Chemung, Cohocton, Genesee. He stopped at Jefferson (now Watkins Glen) at the foot of Seneca Lake and took a boat to Geneva, returning to resume his trip by rail. During his years in Canada, he touched every town along the St. Lawrence River and the northern shore of Lake Ontario that is shown on maps of the period. His trip to the Sault, at the junction of Lakes Superior and Ontario, evolved to a trip down Lake Michigan and eventually his first sight of Galena and the Mississippi. While collecting material for his volumes on New England homes, he traveled to almost every town in Massachusetts, filling at least six sketchbooks with "Houses in East. Mass." and "Houses in Cent. Mass." Views of Charlestown, Plymouth, and North Adams, Massachusetts, done in the 1870's and 80's, show that he never lost interest in drawing the "prospect" of a whole town.

EDWIN WHITEFIELD

The impressive accuracy of Whitefield's views reward him with an important place in American pictorial history. His literal mind, scholarship, and inquisitiveness led to this accuracy. The charm and delicacy of the vast number of sketches, wash drawings, watercolors, oils, and lithographs give him a secure place in American painting and graphic art. The combination of sketchbooks and journals, which he always held the notion to develop for publication, was in keeping with the traditions of the artist-journalists of the nineteenth century. He was formal, withdrawn, private, yet he wholeheartedly camped out in the wilderness of Minnesota for the better part of a year; English-born, he was in spirit an American.

Although he came from England with its tradition of wash water-color and topographical art, he was essentially self-taught. He portrayed a growing America. He was caught up in the enthusiasm of western expansion. He began the movement for the preservation of New England Colonial houses. He exploited the desires of the emerging middle-class for visual embellishments for the walls of their homes, more often than not the representation of something related or recognizable to them. He respected industry in both the economic and human sense of the word; he had energy, drive, and the desire to make money. But above all, he saw his adopted country, and recorded it with a sensitive line. He sketched and painted the rivers, valleys, cities, homes, peninsulas, and simple ponds of this country. He portrayed America with no apologies.

THE ART

View of Albany, N.Y. / From the East. Lithograph printed in 1845 by Lewis & Brown from a drawing by Edwin Whitefield. *Photo courtesy The Mariners Museum, Newport News, Va.*

View of Troy, N.Y. / From the West. Lithograph printed in 1845 by Lewis & Brown from a drawing by Edwin Whitefield and drawn on stone by Whitefield. Photo courtesy The Mariners Museum, Newport News, Va.

View of Harrisburg, Pa. / From the West. Lithograph printed in 1846 by Lewis & Brown from a drawing by Edwin Whitefield. *Photo courtesy the Historical Society of Dauphin County (Pa.).*

View of Newburgh, N.Y. Lithograph drawn from nature and on stone by Whitefield in 1846. Courtesy Print Room, New-York Historical Society.

View of Brooklyn, L.I. / From U.S. Hotel, New York. Lithograph printed in 1846 by Michelin from a drawing by Whitefield and drawn on stone by Whitefield and D. Moody. *Courtesy The Mariners Museum, Newport News, Va.*

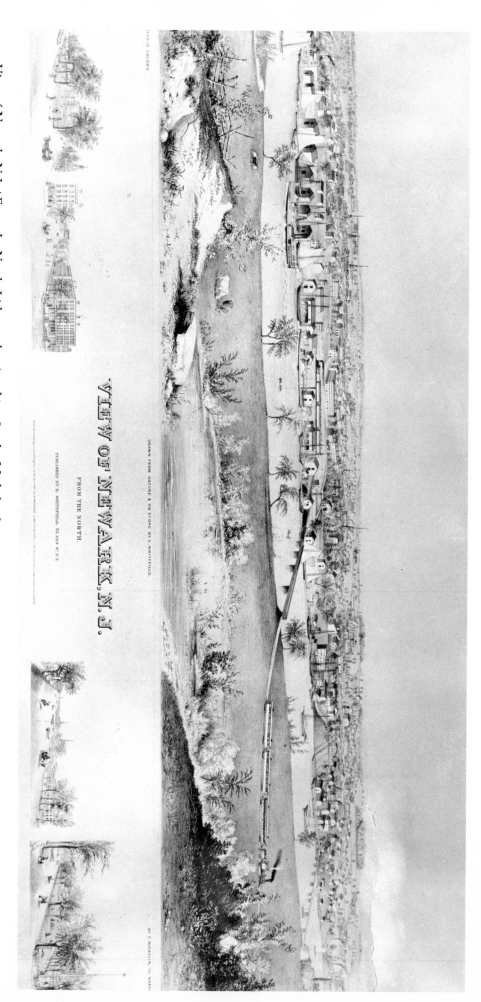

View of Newark, N.J. / From the North. Lithograph printed in 1847 by Michelin from a drawing by Whitefield and drawn on stone by Whitefield. Photo courtesy the New Jersey Historical Society.

View of Baltimore, Md./From Federal Hill. Lithograph printed by Michelin in 1847 from a drawing by Whitefield and "engraved" on stone by Whitefield. *Courtesy Maryland Historical Society.*

View of Rochester, N.Y. / Taken From the Neighborhood of Mount Hope. Lithograph probably printed in 1847 from a drawing by Whitefield and drawn on stone by Whitefield. Courtesy Margaret Woodbury Strong Museum, Rochester.

Poughkeepsie, from the opposite side of the Hudson River. Whitefield published this colored lithograph of a small, attractive New York town in 1852. Photo courtesy Prints Division, The New York Public Library, Astor, Lenox, and Tilden Foundations.

From Durham Terrace, Quebec

From Durham Terrace, Quebec, one of many wash drawings and watercolors which Whitefield painted during his years in Canada. Wash drawing, c. 1853. Photo courtesy the Sigmund Samuel Canadiana Collection, Royal Ontario Museum, Toronto.

FACING PAGE:

Montreal from Mount Royal. Whitefield painted this oil from the drawing which he had done earlier for the lithographed view. He exhibited it in New York City and throughout Canada, in 1854. Courtesy Mr. and Mrs. Jules Loeb, Toronto, Canada. Photo courtesy the National Gallery of Canada, Ottawa.

Starucca Viaduct (Pennsylvania), from the sketchbook entitled "Trip on the Erie R.R. in the Fall of 1854 [1853]." Whitefield's diaries describe this trip through New York and Pennsylvania. Watercolor courtesy M. and M. Karolik Collection, Museum of Fine Arts, Boston.

from Nature, by E. Whitefield 1857.   *Kandotta, M.T. in Oct.ʳ 1857.*

Kandotta, M. T. in Oct. 1857, Whitefield's home in Minnesota. *Watercolor courtesy*
M. and M. Karolik Collection, Museum of Fine Arts, Boston.

Windows narrow
nearly black
Pigeon Cove
The Old Castle
Old clapboards in front
much worn & broken
narrow windows
windows narrow
rocks
Poles
weeds
road to Quarry
This is a little back of Main St. near the P.O.
Road to Quarry

Pigeon Cove / The Old Castle. Wash drawing for *The Homes of our Forefathers in Massachusetts,* by Whitefield, published in 1879. *Photo courtesy Print Department, Boston Public Library.*

"Flower Piece" was the term that Whitefield aptly used to describe his colorful, stylized compositions of wild flowers done in later years. This decorative and tightly constructed bouquet has delicate tints among the bright colors. *Private collection*.

Boston from Parker Hill, around 1866. Watercolor showing the Back Bay of Boston built up as far as Berkeley Street. *Private collection.*

A South-East View of Ye Great Town of Boston in New England in America. Lithograph facsimile, of the rare Price-Burgis engraving of 1743, commissioned by Josiah Quincy, Mayor of Boston in 1848. *Courtesy Charles E. Mason Collection, Boston Athenaeum.*

View of Boston in 1848./ From East Boston./White-field's Original Views of American Cities No. 9. Lithograph printed in 1848 by Whitefield & Smith, from a drawing by Whitefield. Drawn on stone by C. W. Burton. *Courtesy Charles E. Mason Collection, Boston Athenaeum.*

View of Buffalo, N.Y. / From the Old Lighthouse. Lithograph printed by Michelin,
probably in 1848, from a drawing by Whitefield done in 1846. *Photo courtesy
The Mariners Museum, Newport News, Va.*

View of Cincinnati, Ohio. / From Covington, Ky. Lithograph printed in 1848 by Jones
& Newman from a drawing by Whitefield and "engraved" on stone by Whitefield.
Photo courtesy The Mariners Museum, Newport News, Va.

View of Providence R.I. From the North. 1849. Whitefield's Original Views of American Cities, No. 12. Lithograph printed in 1849 by Michelin from a drawing by Whitefield and put on stone by C. W. Burton. *Courtesy, Charles E. Mason Collection, Boston Athenaeum.*

View of Providence R.I. From the South. 1849. Whitefield's Original Views of American Cities, No. 12. Lithograph printed by Michelin in 1849 from a drawing by Whitefield and put on stone by C. W. Burton. (The double use of No. 12 is Whitefield's mistake.) *Courtesy, Charles E. Mason Collection, Boston, Athenaeum.*

View of Portland, Me. / From the Cape Elizabeth Side. Lithograph printed by Michelin in 1849 from a drawing by Whitefield and "engraved" on stone by Whitefield. *Courtesy Maine Historical Society*.

View of Hartford, Ct. / From the Deaf and Dumb Asylum. Lithograph printed in 1849 by Michelin from a drawing by Whitefield and "engraved" on stone by Whitefield. *Courtesy Connecticut Historical Society.*

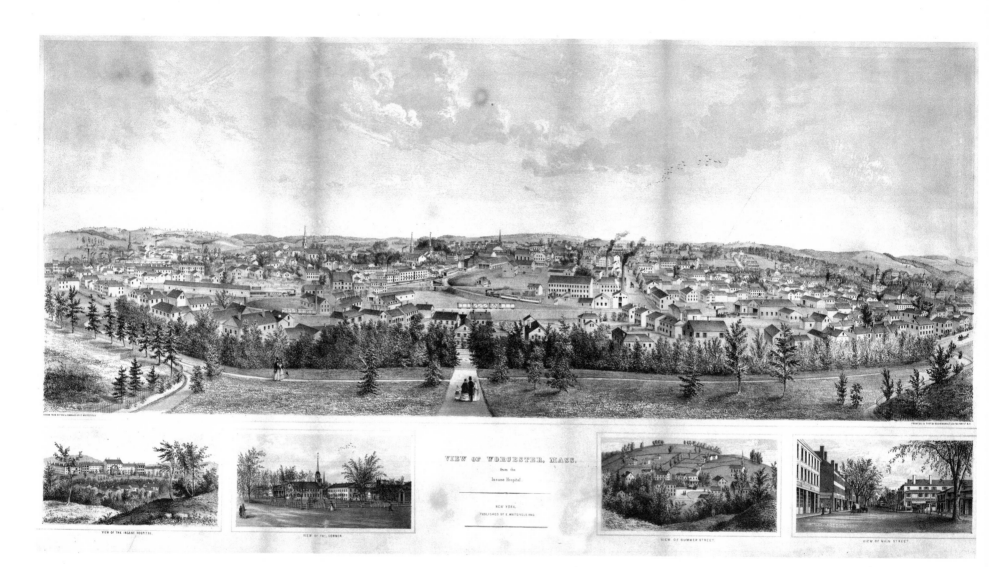

View of Worcester, Mass. / From the Insane Hospital. Lithograph printed by Buchanan
& Co. in 1849 from a drawing by Whitefield and "engraved" on stone by Whitefield.
Courtesy, Charles E. Mason Collection, Boston Athenaeum.

View of Salem, Mass. Lithograph printed by Michelin in 1849 from a drawing by
Whitefield and "engraved" on stone by Whitefield. *Courtesy Essex Institute.*

Panoramic Views of Philadelphia. / From the State House. / North View / Looking Across Chestnut St. Towards Spring Garden, Northern Liberties and Kensington. Lithograph printed by Endicott & Co., probably in 1850, from a drawing by Whitefield. Photos courtesy the Print and Picture Department, Free Library of Philadelphia.

Panoramic Views of Philadelphia. / From the State House. South View / Looking Towards Navy Yard, Southwark and Moyamensing.

*Panoramic Views of Philadelphia. / From the State House. East View / Looking Down
Chestnut St. Across the Delaware—Camden, N.J. in the Distance.*

Panoramic Views of Philadelphia. / From the State House. West View / Looking up Chestnut St. Towards West Philadelphia.

[New York City from the Harbor.] Steel engraving, possibly by Robert Hinshelwood, after a drawing by Whitefield, done probably in 1850. *Photo courtesy Canadiana Department, Royal Ontario Museum.* (See pp. 90–91 for enlargement.)

Facing page, top: [New York from Williamsburgh, L.I.] Steel engraving, possibly by Robert Hinshelwood, after a drawing by Whitefield. *Photo courtesy Canadiana Department, Royal Ontario Museum.* Facing page, bottom: [New York from Weehawken, N.J.] Steel engraving, possibly by Robert Hinshelwood, after a drawing by Whitefield. *Photo courtesy Map and Print Room, New-York Historical Society.*

[New York City from the Harbor.] (Enlarged view of illustration on p. 88.)

VIEW OF SALEM, MASS.

VIEW OF LYNN, MASS.

VIEW OF BEVERLY, MASS.

VIEW OF DANVERS, MASS.

View of Salem, Mass.; View of Lynn, Mass.; View of Beverly, Mass.; and *View of Danvers, Mass.* Lithographs printed on one sheet by Endicott & Co., probably in 1850, after drawings by Whitefield. *Courtesy Essex Institute.*

View of Pittsburg, Pa. Lithograph printed probably in 1850 by Hudson & Smith from
a drawing by Whitefield and signed on the stone by Whitefield. *Private collection.*

View of Trenton, N.J. From Morrisville, Pa. Lithograph printed by Endicott & Co. after drawings by Whitefield and drawn on stone by Whitefield. *Photo courtesy The Mariners Museum, Newport News, Va.*

View of Wilmington, Del. / From the Newport Road. Lithograph printed in 1852 by
Endicott & Co. after a drawing by Whitefield and drawn on stone by Whitefield. *Photo
courtesy Historical Society of Delaware.*

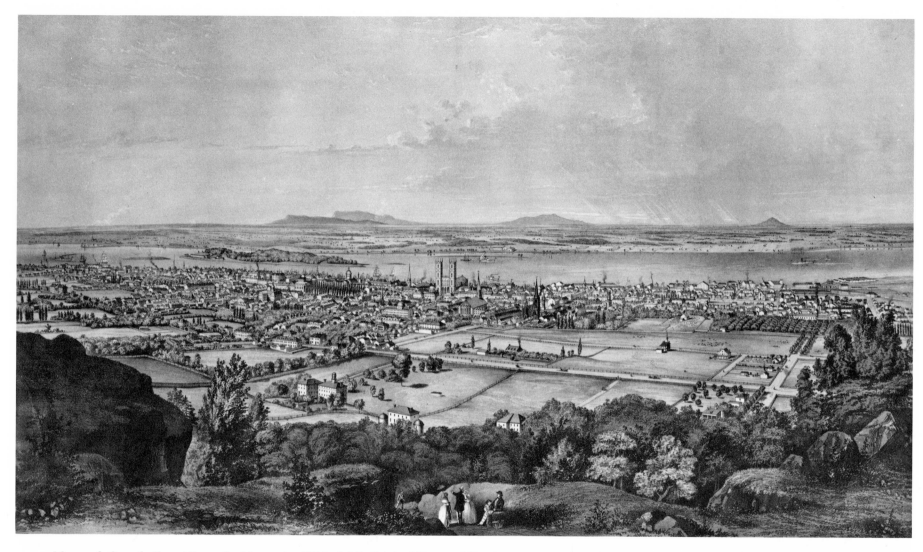

Montreal, Canada East. / From the Mountain. Whitefield's Original Views of North American Cities No. 25. Lithograph printed by Endicott in 1852 after a drawing by Whitefield. *Photo courtesy Public Archives of Canada, Ottawa.*

Montreal, Canada East./From the Mountain. Whitefield's Original Views of North American Cities No. 25. Although this lithograph was printed probably in 1855, from a different drawing, the lettering was not changed although there are two additions and some relettering. Whitefield probably drew this second edition on the stone. He also did an oil painting of this scene, reproduced in the color plate section. *Photo courtesy Print Department, New York Public Library.*

View of Williamsburgh, L.I. / From Grand St., N.Y. Whitefield's Original Views of North American Cities No. 26. Lithograph printed in 1852 by Endicott & Co. from a drawing by Whitefield. *Courtesy Print Room, New-York Historical Society.*

Quebec. / From Beauport. Whitefield's Views of North American Cities No. 26.
Lithograph printed by Endicott & Co. in 1852 from a drawing by Whitefield. (The
double use of No. 26 is again Whitefield's mistake). *Photo courtesy Prints Division,
Astor, Lenox, and Tilden Foundations, New York Public Library.*

Taghanic Fall / (215 feet high) / Near Ithaca Tomkins Co. / N.Y. Lithograph printed in 1854 by Endicott & Co. after a drawing by White-field. On stone by D. Glasgow, *Photo courtesy Prints Division, The New York Public Library, Astor, Lenox and Tilden Foundations.*

Hamilton, Canada West. / From the Mountain. Whitefield's Original Views of North American Cities No. 29. Lithograph printed in 1854 *by Endicott & Co. after a drawing by Whitefield. Photo courtesy Public Archives of Canada, Ottawa.*

Toronto, Canada West. / From the Top of the Jail. Whitefield's Original Views of North American Cities No. 30. Lithograph printed by Endicott & Co. in 1854 from a drawing by Whitefield. *Photo courtesy Canadiana Department, Royal Ontario Museum.*

Kingston, Canada West. / From Fort Henry. Whitefield's Original Views of North American Cities No. 33. Lithograph printed in 1855 from a drawing by Whitefield. *Photo courtesy Canadiana Department, Royal Ontario Museum.*

Ottawa City, Canada West./(Late Bytown). Whitefield's Original Views of North American Cities No. 34. Lithograph published by Whitefield in 1855 from his original drawing. *Photo courtesy Public Archives of Canada, Ottawa.*

Ottawa City, Canada West./Lower Town. Whitefield's Original Views of North American Cities No. 35. Lithograph published by Whitefield in 1855 from his original drawing. *Photo courtesy Public Archives of Canada, Ottawa.*

London, Canada West. Whitefield's Original Views of North American Cities No. 36.
Lithograph published by Whitefield in 1855 from his original drawing. *Photo courtesy
Public Archives of Canada, Ottawa.*

View of Galena, Ill. Whitefield's Original Views of North American Cities No. 37.
Lithograph published by Endicott & Co. in 1856 after a drawing by Whitefield. *Photo courtesy Prints Division, The New York Public Library, Astor, Lenox and Tilden Foundations.*

View of Niagara Falls. Whitefield's Original Views of North American Scenery, No. 38.
Lithograph printed by Endicott, probably in 1856, from a drawing by Whitefield.
Photo courtesy Public Archives of Canada, Ottawa.

View of St. Anthony, Minneapolis, and St. Anthony Falls / From Cheever's Tower.
1857. Lithograph printed by Endicott in 1857 from a drawing by Whitefield. *Photo courtesy Minnesota Historical Society.*

View of Illinois and Michigan Central Depot &c. Whitefield's Views of Chicago.
Lithograph printed by Chas. Shober in 1860 from a drawing by E. Whitefield. *Courtesy Essex Institute.*

View of Clark & Wells St. Bridges. E. Whitefields Views of Chicago. Lithograph printed
by Chas. Shober in 1861 after a drawing by Whitefield. *Courtesy Essex Institute.*

Views of Michigan Ave &c. / From Sturges & Buckingham's Elevator. E. Whitefields
Views of Chicago. Lithograph printed in 1861 by Chas. Shober after a drawing by
Whitefield. *Courtesy Essex Institute.*

View of Sherman House / Court House &c. Whitefields Views of Chicago. Lithograph
printed in 1861 by Chas. Shober after a drawing by Whitefield. *Courtesy Essex Institute.*

View of Rush St. Bridge &c. E. Whitefields Views of Chicago. Lithograph printed in
1861 by Chas. Shober after a drawing by Whitefield. *Courtesy Essex Institute.*

View of the Tremont House &c. Whitefield's Views of Chicago. Lithograph printed in 1861 by Chas. Shober from a drawing by Whitefield. *Photo courtesy Chicago Historical Society.*

Michigan Terrace, / Michigan Avenue. Whitefields Views of Chicago. Lithograph printed in 1863 by Chas. Shober from a drawing by Whitefield. *Courtesy Print Department, Boston Public Library.*

View of the Public Garden & Boston Common. Lithograph printed in 1866 by J. H.
Bufford from a drawing by Whitefield. *Courtesy Boston Athenaeum.*

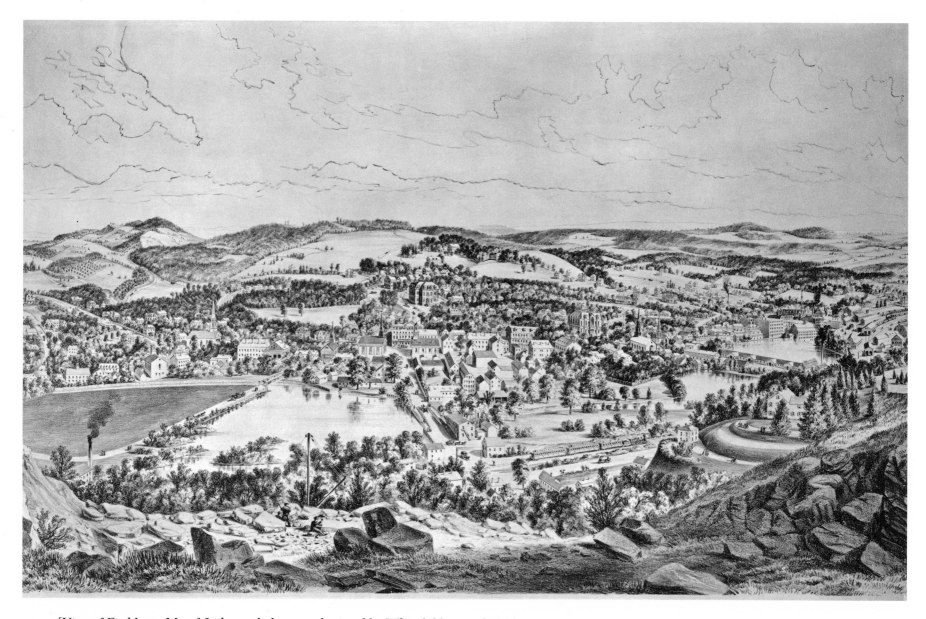

[View of Fitchburg, Mass.] Lithograph drawn and printed by Whitefield, around 1866.
Private collection.

View of Portsmouth, N.H. / on July 4th, 1873. / From the head of Mt. Vernon Street . . .
Sepia photograph of a drawing by Whitefield. *Courtesy Strawbery Banke, Inc.,*
Portsmouth, N.H.

View of Portsmouth, N.H. / On July 4th 1873. From the head of North Pond. Sepia
photograph from a drawing by Whitefield. *Courtesy Strawbery Banke, Inc.,
Portsmouth, N.H.*

Malden, Mass. Sepia photograph published in 1875 by Whitefield from his original drawing. *Courtesy Print Department, Boston Public Library.*

Newburyport, Mass. in the year 1876. / From Belleville Church. Sepia photograph published by Whitefield from his original drawing. *Courtesy American Antiquarian Society.*

View of Worcester, Mass. / From Worcester Academy, Union Hill. Sepia photograph published in 1876 by Whitefield from his original drawing. *Courtesy American Antiquarian Society.*

View of Lowell, Mass. / From Centerville. Sepia photograph published by Whitefield in 1876 from his original drawing. *Photo courtesy Canadiana Department, Royal Ontario Museum.*

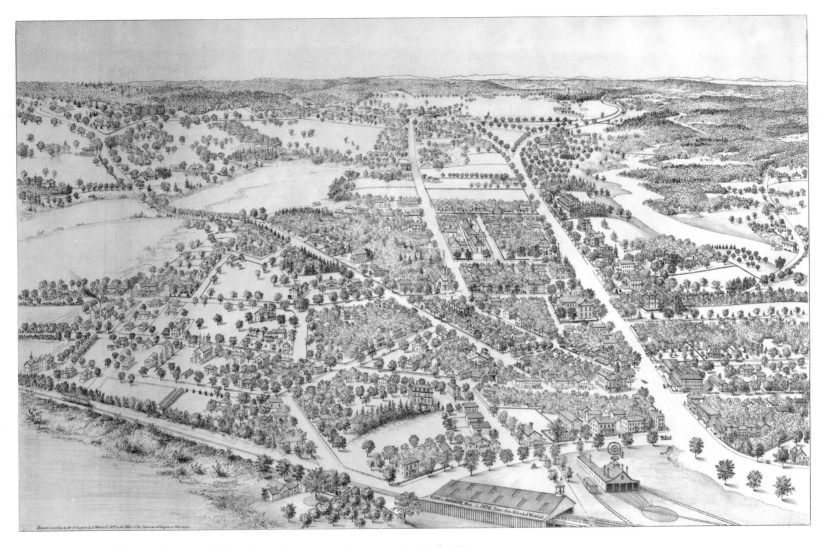

View of Dedham, Mass. in 1876. Lithograph drawn, printed, and published by
Whitefield in 1876. *Courtesy Print Department, Boston Public Library.*

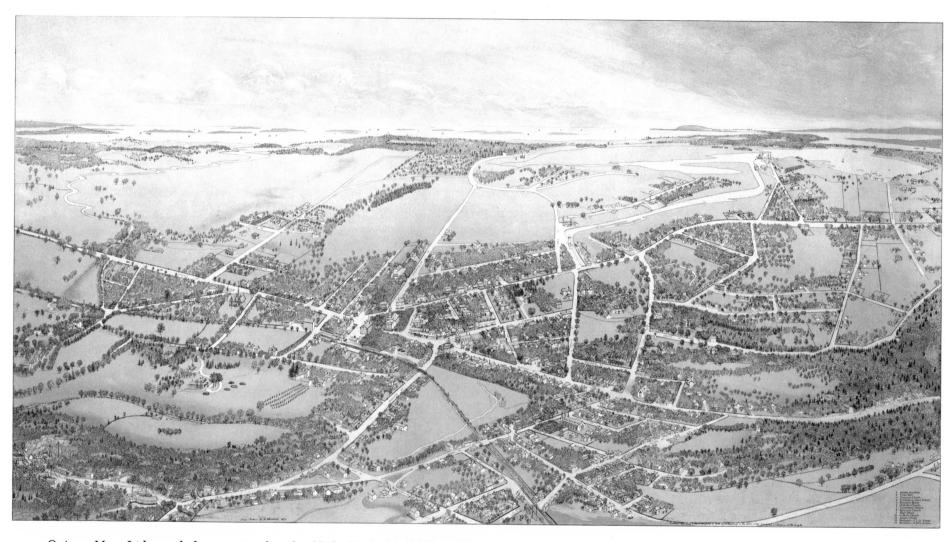

Quincy, Mass. Lithograph drawn, printed, and published by Whitefield in 1878.
Courtesy Print Department, Boston Public Library.

Appendix: The Works of Whitefield

1 List of Exhibitions and Awards

1842 N.Y. State Agricultural Society / for Floral Painting.
1842 American Institute of New York. Best Painting of Fruit.
1852 National Academy of Design.
    269. *View of the Hook Mountain, near Nyack, N.Y.*
1853 National Academy of Design.
    208. *View of Montreal.*
    288. *Part of Fort Ticonderoga.*
    290. *Falls of the Chaudiere, Canada East.*
1854 National Academy of Design.
    247. *View of Hamilton.*
    Upper Canada Provincial Exhibition, Cobourg. (October ?).

1855 Paris, Canada West, Town Fair. July, 1855.
    Views of Hamilton and Toronto.
    Upper Canada Provincial Exhibition, Coburg. October 12–15.
    Awarded five prizes. Exhibited *Montreal.*
1856 Toronto exhibition of his own works, February 21–March 8.
    Paris, Canada West, Town Fair. July, 1856.
    Awarded five prizes.
    Territorial Fair in Minneapolis. October 9, 1856.

Note: The information under the three entries for the National Academy of Design is taken from the *NAD Exhibition Record, 1826–1860*, ed. by M. Bartlett Cowdrey, New York, 1943.

Silver medal from the American Institute of New York, awarded to E. Whitefield in 1845 for the best painting of fruit. *Courtesy Print Department, Boston Public Library.*

2 Oil Paintings

In addition to the paintings exhibited at the National Academy of Design in 1852, 1853, and 1854, which were probably oils, there are some in private and public collections:

Mrs. Frances Bond, Wellesley, Massachusetts:
    Lake Winnepesaukee. 29¼ x 20½ (sight).
    Lake, with hotel and sidewheeler (Winnepesaukee, with the *Mount Washington*?). 13½ x 19⅜ (sight).
    Landscape, signed E. Whitefield, 1885. 20½ x 29¼ (sight).

Boston Public Library, Boston, Massachusetts:
    Red Hill (Near Center Harbor, N.H.). 12¼ x 18½.
    Great Falls of the Ottawa, Canada. 16 x 20.
    Falls of St. Anne, below Quebec, Canada (signed on rev.). 22 x 14.
    Untitled landscape. 14 x 22.
    Untitled landscape. 9¼ x 12¼.
    Untitled landscape. 13¾ x 9½.

Charles D. Childs, Stow, Massachusetts: *Susquehanna.*

Mr. and Mrs. Jules Loeb, Toronto, Canada: *View of Montreal,* 1854.

Old Print Shop, New York: *Falls at Ithaca.*

Sigmund Samuel Canadiana Collection, Royal Ontario Museum, Toronto, Canada:
    Falls of the Montmorenci, Quebec, in the Winter. 9¼ x 13⅛.
    Falls of Montmorenci From the Point Levi Side. 17 x 22½.

Peter Winkworth, Montreal and London, England: *View of Montreal.*

There are also references to oil paintings in the Whitefield diaries:
    Aug. 1842   Entrance to the Highlands, from the Fishkill side.
    Sept. 1852   Taughanic Falls.
    Oct. 1852   Chaudiere Falls.
    Jan. 1853   Falls of La Puce.
    May 1855   Mr. Kerr's house.
    July 1855   Toronto.
    Nov. 1856   View of Rapid Water ("which answers well").
    Dec. 1856   Minnehaha.

J. Russell Harper, in *Early Painters and Engravers of Canada,* (Toronto, 1970) refers to an oil, now unlocated: *Tadoussac.*

3 *Lithographs*

The bulk of Whitefield's lithographs (plus seven sepia photoreproductions and one steel engraving) have here been divided into two categories:

    I   A numbered chronological list of views of cities and scenery that are part of a series.

    II   A numbered chronological list of miscellaneous single lithographs.

For clarity in reference, numbering continues from one section to the next.

Several problems arose in the process of arriving at a correlation between the numbered and the unnumbered prints in *Whitefield's Original Views of (North) American Cities (Scenery).* Most awkward was a misnumbering of two views. Both *Williamsburgh, L.I.,* and *Quebec, From Beauport,* were given "Nº 26"; and the second edition of *Montreal, Canada East,* though a different stone, used the same lettering as the first edition, and therefore, though published in 1855, reads "Entered . . . 1852."

Exact wording from the prints is used; inconsistencies are Whitefield's own.

Measurements are of the image only; they include neither tint-line borders nor lettering. Date of depiction is given if it differs from date of publication.

Twelve institutions which contain a number of Whitefield works are referred to by initials:

AAS	American Antiquarian Society, Worcester, Massachusetts
BA	Boston Athenaeum, Boston, Massachusetts
BPL	Boston Public Library, Boston, Massachusetts
CHS	Chicago Historical Society, Chicago, Illinois
EI	Essex Institute, Salem, Massachusetts
MHS	Minnesota Historical Society, St. Paul, Minnesota
MMNN	Mariners Museum, Newport News, Virginia
NYHS	New-York Historical Society, New York, New York
NYPL	New York Public Library, New York, New York (Stokes Collection)
PAC	Public Archives of Canada, Ottawa
ROM	Royal Ontario Museum (Canadiana Department Collection), Toronto, Canada
SSTB	State Street Bank and Trust Company, Boston, Massachusetts

LITHOGRAPHS IN SERIES

North American Scenery

Whitefield's first series was lithographed in part by F. Michelin (four views), and E. Jones & G. W. Newman (eight views). The remaining sixteen views do not identify the lithographer. A bound volume of the twenty-eight published views, though out of order, and four pamphlets complete enough for identification purposes (some are missing covers and/or title pages) in the collection at the New-York Historical Society are the basis for the list that follows.

Some prints have "Drawn from Nature by E. Whitefield" below the print on the left, with the name of the lithographer to the right. Others have attribution centered between the print and the lower tint border. Not all the views have a tint border, however. Some lettering is in script, some in block letters. All views are approximately 6″ x 9″. The title page reads:

NORTH AMERICAN SCENERY
Faithfully Delineated
In a series of illustrative views,
From original drawings, taken on the spot
by E. Whitefield.
The literary department under the superintendence of
John Keese, Esq.

Plan of publication. A *Part* will be published *punctually* on the first of every month. Each *Part* will contain FOUR ENGRAVINGS printed in tints, and eight pages of illustrative text. The work will be beautifully printed on medium Quarto, with new type, and will be completed in Twenty-Four *Parts*, at TWENTY-FIVE CENTS each.

New York: Published by H. Long & Brother
No. 32 Ann Street
Sold by all the periodical agents in the country
Entered.... 1846, by E. Whitefield.... New York

(The parts were issued in seven monthly installments, beginning in January, 1846.)

Part 1
1 *Country Seat, near Yonkers, Hudson River.*
2 *Cohoes Falls, Mohawk River, New York.*
3 *View on the Ohio River, at the Pa. & Ohio State Line.*
4 *View on the Susquehanna near Harrisburgh, Pa.*

Part 2
5 *View near Norwich, Ct.*
   Printed by F. Michelin, III, Nassau St.
6 *View of the Caatskill Mts. from Upper Red Hook.*
   Printed by F. Michelin, N.Y.
7 *View from Peekskill, N.Y. (Regatta).*
   Printed by F. Michelin, N.Y.
8 *West Point & Fort Putnam from the east.*

Part 3
9 *Residence of S.S. Haldeman Esq. near Columbia, Pa.*
10 *Part of Steubenville, Ohio.*
11 *Otsego Lake, N.Y.*
12 *Sunny Side, Residence of Washington Irving, Esq.*
   Printed by E. Jones & G. W. Newman.

Part 4
13 *View on the Conestoga, near Lancaster, Pᵃ*
   Printed by E. Jones & G. W. Newman, N.Y.
14 *Tivoli, or Upper Red Hook, Hudson River, N.Y.*
   Printed by E. Jones & G. W. Newman.
15 *Ice Cutting on Crystall Lake, near New Rochelle, N.Y.*
   Printed by E. Jones & G. W. Newman.

16 *Falls of the Yantic near Norwich, Connect.*

Part 5
17 *Fountain Park near Philadelphia, Residence of A. McMakin, Esq.*
18 *View near Croton, N.Y. Hudson River.*
19 *Village of Essex, N.Y. Lake Champlain.*
20 *The Beverly House, (Arnold's Head Quarters when in command of West Point.), Hudson River, N.Y.*

Part 6
21 *The Smith House (Scene of the Conference between Arnold and Andre) Haverstraw, N.Y.*
22 *Monument of John Paulding. (One of the Captors of Andre) near Peekskill, N.Y.*
23 *Falls on the Lackawana, Pᵃ near Tunkhannock, Pᵃ*
   Printed by F. Michelin, III, Nassau St., N.Y.
24 *View of Harrisburg, Pᵃ from the S.W.*

Part 7
25 *Falls of the Genesee, Rochester, N.Y.*
   Printed by E. Jones & G. W. Newman.
26 *Saratoga Lake, N.Y.*
   Printed by E. Jones & G. W. Newman.
27 *Residence of R. P. Parrot, Esq., Cold Spring, N.Y.*
   Printed by E. Jones & G. W. Newman.
28 *View in the Backwoods, Ohio.*
   Printed by E. Jones & G. W. Newman.

North American Cities and Scenery

29 VIEW OF ALBANY N.Y. / From the East.
From an Original Drawing by E. Whitefield.
Lewis & Brown, Lith. New York.
[34 numbered references in 6 columns below image]
[1845]
17 x 24¼, tinted
Collection: MMNN

30 VIEW OF TROY, N.Y. / From the West.
Drawn from Nature by E. Whitefield.
[signed on stone:] E. Whitefield

Lith. of Lewis & Brown, New-York.
Published by Lewis & Brown, 272 Pearl St. New York.
Entered . . . 1845 by Lewis & Brown & E. Whitefield . . .
[4 references below image]
16�]/16 x 26¼, tinted
Collections: MMNN, Rensselaer County Historical Society, Troy Public
   Library

31 VIEW OF HARRISBURG, PA. / From the West.
Drawn from Nature by E. Whitefield.
Lith. by Lewis & Brown, 37 John St. N.Y.
Published by Lewis & Brown, 37 John St. New York
[1846]
16½ x 23, tinted
Collection: Historical Society of Dauphin County

32 VIEW OF NEWBURGH, N.Y.
From Nature & on Stone by E. Whitefield.
Entered . . . 1846 by E. Whitefield.
[6 references below image]
14 x 23⅝
Collections: MMNN, NYHS, NYPL

33 VIEW OF BROOKLYN, L.I. / From U.S. Hotel, New York.
Drawn from Nature & on Stone by E. Whitefield.
Printed in colors by F. Michelin, III, Nassau St.
Entered . . . 1846 by E. Whitefield . . .
14¾ x 36, tinted
Collections: CHS, MMNN, NYHS, NYPL
NYHS also owns the original watercolor, 8¼ x 40

34 VIEW OF NEWARK, N.J. / From the North.
Drawn from Nature & on Stone by E. Whitefield.
Printed in colors by F. Michelin, III, Nassau St. N.Y.
Entered . . . 1847 by E. Whitefield . . .
Published by E. Whitefield, 32 Ann St. N.Y.
[date depicted: 1845–6]
[4 small views below main image, each 3⅛ x 6:]
   View of Upper Park.
   View in Market St.
   View in Broad St.
   View in Lower Park.

17¾ x 35¾
Collections: MMNN, New Jersey Historical Society

35 VIEW OF BALTIMORE, MD. / From Federal Hill.
Drawn from Nature and Engraved by E. Whitefield.
Printed in colors by F. Michelin, III, Nassau St. N.Y.
Pubd. by E. Whitefield, 32 Ann St. N.York.
Entered . . . 1847 by E. Whitefield . . .
[date depicted: 1846]
17⅛ x 40⅛
Collection: Maryland Historical Society

36 VIEW OF ROCHESTER, N.Y. / Taken From the Neighborhood of
      Mount Hope.
Drawn from Nature on Stone by E. Whitefield.
Printed in colors by F. Michelin, III, Nassau St. N.Y.
[14 references below image]
[probably 1847]
14¼ x 32⅝ [sight]
Collections: Rochester Historical Society, Rochester Public Library,
   Margaret Woodbury Strong Museum, University of Rochester:
   Rush Rhees Library

37 VIEW OF BOSTON IN 1848. / From East Boston.
WHITEFIELD'S ORIGINAL VIEWS OF AMERICAN CITIES No. 9
From a Drawing by E. Whitefield.
C. Burton, Delt.
Boston, published by Whitefield & Smith.
Entered . . . 1848 . . .
Note: The Mariners Museum's impression has 19 numbered references
   in blue tint below the image. The view was also issued with a gray tint.
   In 1889, Whitefield made a smaller photoreproduction of it.
19 x 43¾, tinted
Collections: BA, BPL, Bostonian Society, CHS, EI, MMNN, Massachusetts
   Historical Society, NYHS, ROM, PAC, SStB

38 VIEW OF BUFFALO, N.Y. / From the Old Lighthouse.
Drawn from Nature & on Stone by E. Whitefield.
Printed in colors by F. Michelin, III, Nassau St. N.Y.
Entered . . . 184• by E. Whitefield . . .
[date depicted: 1846; date issued, prob. 1848]
[15 numbered references in 2 columns below image; 14 named

steamboats, 3 named schooners]

14¼ x 37

Collections: Buffalo and Erie County Historical Society, MMNN, NYHS, ROM

39 VIEW OF CINCINNATI, OHIO. / From Covington, Ky.
Drawn from Nature by E. Whitefield.
Engraved by E. Whitefield.
Printed in colors by Jones & Newman, 128 Fulton St. N.Y.
Published by E. Whitefield, 32 Ann St. N.Y.
Entered . . . 1848 by E. Whitefield . . .
[date depicted: 1846]

16½ x 37⅞
Collection: MMNN

40 VIEW OF PROVIDENCE R.I. FROM THE SOUTH. 1849.
WHITEFIELD'S ORIGINAL VIEWS OF AMERICAN CITIES, No. 12
From a Drawing by E. Whitefield.
Drawn on Stone by C. W. Burton.
Printed by F. Michelin, III, Nassau St. N.Y.
Published by Whitefield & Smith.
Entered . . . 1849, by E. Whitefield.

16⅛ x 37¾, tinted
Collections: AAS, BA, CHS, MMNN, PAC, Providence Athenaeum

41 VIEW OF PROVIDENCE R.I. FROM THE NORTH. 1849.
WHITEFIELD'S ORIGINAL VIEWS OF AMERICAN CITIES, No. 12
From a Drawing by E. Whitefield.
Drawn on Stone by C. W. Burton.
Printed by F. Michelin, III, Nassau St. N.Y.
Published by Whitefield & Smith.
Entered . . . 1849 by E. Whitefield . . .
Note: Both these Providence views were printed with the same letter
stone; in many cases, the "S" and "u" in "South" were erased, and "N"
and "r" substituted, as minute examination revealed.

16⅛ x 37⅝, tinted
Collections: AAS, BA, MMNN, NYHS, Providence Athenaeum

42 VIEW OF PORTLAND, ME. / From the Cape Elizabeth Side.
Drawn from Nature by E. Whitefield.
Engraved by E. Whitefield.
Printed in colors by Jones & Newman, 128 Fulton St. N.Y.

Published by Whitefield & Smith, 128 Fulton St. N.Y.

16½ x 36
Collections: Maine Historical Society, Portland Public Library

43 VIEW OF HARTFORD, CT. / From the / Deaf and Dumb Asylum.
Drawn from Nature & Engraved by E. Whitefield.
Printed by F. Michelin, III, Nassau St. N.Y.
New York. / Published by E. Whitefield. / 1849.
[4 small views below main image, each 4 x 7¼:]
    View of the Charter Oak.
    View of the Deaf and Dumb Asylum.
    View of the [Trinity] Colleges.
    View of the State House . . .

18 x 35⅛, tinted
Collection: Connecticut Historical Society

44 VIEW OF WORCESTER, MASS. / From the / Insane Hospital.
Drawn from Nature & Engraved by E. Whitefield.
Printed in tint by Buchanan & Co. 128 Fulton St. N.Y.
New York. / Published by E. Whitefield. 1849.
[4 small views below main image, each 3½ x 6⅞:]
    View of the Insane Hospital.
    View of the Common.
    View of Summer Street.
    View of Main Street.

14¼ x 36¾
Collections: AAS, BA

45 VIEW OF SALEM, MASS.
Drawn from Nature & Engraved by E. Whitefield.
Printed by F. Michlin [Michelin], III, Nassau St. N.Y.
Published by E. Whitefield, New-York.
Entered . . . 1849 by E. Whitefield . . .
Note: This print was issued in two versions—with differing tints.

15 x 38½
Collection: EI

46 VIEW OF TROY, N.Y. IN 1848 / From Mount Ida.
[See Stokes and Haskell, *American Historical Prints*: Sarony & Major,
    N.Y. 39.8 x 22.8 1850. p. 157.]
[date issued: probably 1850]
Collection: Avis and Rockwell Gardiner, Stamford, Connecticut, have a
    tracing on three sheets glued together, 8⅞ x 39.

47 PANORAMIC VIEWS OF PHILADELPHIA / From the State House.
NORTH VIEW / Looking Across Chestnut St. Towards Spring Garden,
  Northern Liberties, and Kensington.
EAST VIEW / Looking Down Chestnut St. Across the Delaware—
  Camden, N.J. in the Distance.
WEST VIEW / Looking up Chestnut St. Towards West Philadelphia.
SOUTH VIEW / Looking Towards Navy Yard, Southwark and
  Moyamensing.
Drawn from Nature by E. Whitefield.
Lith. of Wm. Endicott & Co., N.Y.
[1850]
Each 10½ x 19
Collections: Free Library of Philadelphia, Library of Congress,
  Martin P. Snyder, Philadelphia, Pennsylvania

48 [NEW YORK]
[Survives only in proof; line engraving probably by Robert Hinshelwood
  after drawings by E. Whitefield. Upper views, of New York from
  Williamsburgh, Long Island, and from Weehawken, New Jersey, each
  10⅛ x 23¾; lower view, of New York from the Harbor, 15 x 49⅜
  inches. Listed in Stokes, *Iconography of Manhattan Island,* vol. 3,
  p. 894, under "List of Supplementary Prints" as possibly by Robert
  Havell.]
[1850]
Collections: NYHS, ROM

49 VIEW OF SALEM, MASS.
VIEW OF LYNN, MASS.
  Arranged by E. Whitefield.
  from a Daguerrotype by S. H. Whitmore.
VIEW OF BEVERLY, MASS.
VIEW OF DANVERS, MASS.
Drawn from Nature by E. Whitefield.
Printed by Wm. Endicott & Co., N.Y.
Salem, 8 x 33
Lynn, 6⁹⁄₁₆ x 29
Beverly, 4¾ x 16
Danvers, 4¾ x 16¼
[1850]
Collections (the whole sheet; other institutions have one or more of the
  separated views): EI, NYPL, SSTB

50 VIEW OF PITTSBURG, PA .
Drawn by E. Whitefield.
Pubd. by Hudson & Smith, Fulton, St. N.Y.
[On stone:] E. Whitefield.
[probably 1850]
17¾ x 37, tinted
Collection: Raymond C. Wright, Pittsburgh, Pa.

51 VIEW OF TRENTON, N.J. FROM MORRISVILLE, PA.
Drawn from Nature and on Stone by E. Whitefield.
Lith. of Wm. Endicott & Co. N. York.
[Above main image:] View of the Trenton Cottages, R.R. Station, &c.
  taken from Cunningham's Tremont House. 4⅛ x 9½
[Below main image, five views:]
  New Presbyterian Church &c. / Warren St. 5¾ x 3⅜
  State St. From the City Hall. 5¾ x 3⅜
  Academy and Public School. 3½ x 3½
  Quintin's Washington Retreat & Bottom and Co's works on
    the Assanopink. 5¾ x 3⅜
  City Hall, &c. Looking up Green St. 6 x 3⅜
[27 references below main image]
[1851]
Main view 21⅞ x 34¼, tinted
Collections: MMNN, New Jersey Historical Society, NYPL

52 [PATERSON, N.J.]
[No surviving examples known.]
[probably 1851]

53 VIEW OF WILMINGTON, DEL. / From the Newport Road.
Drawn from Nature and on Stone by E. Whitefield.
Lith. of Endicott & Co. N.Y.
Entered . . . 1852, by E. Whitefield.
16 x 32½, tinted
Collection: Historical Society of Delaware

54 MONTREAL, CANADA EAST. / From the Mountain.
WHITEFIELD'S ORIGINAL VIEWS OF NORTH AMERICAN CITIES No. 25
Drawn from Nature by E. Whitefield.
Lith. of Endicott & Co. N.Y.
Montreal, published by E. Whitefield Gt. St. James St.
[1852]
[20 references below image]

19¾ x 34¾
Collection: McCord Museum, PAC

55 VIEW OF WILLIAMSBURGH, L.I. / From Grand St., N.Y.
WHITEFIELD'S ORIGINAL VIEWS OF NORTH AMERICAN CITIES No. 26
Drawn from Nature by E. Whitefield.
Lith. of Endicott & Co. New York
Entered . . . 1852 by I. Prindle . . . New York
[24 references below image]
[Note: Both this view and that of Quebec, which follows, were numbered
    26; Whitefield was working on these and views of Montreal and
    Poughkeepsie simultaneously, which probably led to the confusion.]
16 x 33⅝
Collections: CHS, MMNN, NYHS

56 QUEBEC. / FROM BEAUPORT.
WHITEFIELD'S VIEWS OF NORTH AMERICAN CITIES No. 26
Drawn from Nature by E. Whitefield.
Lith. of Endicott & Co., New York.
Published by E. Whitefield, Quebec.
Entered . . . 1852 by E. Whitefield . . . New York.
[20 references below image]
19⅜ x 34⅛
Collections: McCord Museum (Montreal), MMNN, NYPL, PAC, Musée
    du Quebec, ROM

57 POUGHKEEPSIE / From the opposite side of the Hudson River.
WHITEFIELD'S VIEWS OF NORTH AMERICAN CITIES No. 27
Drawn from Nature and on Stone by E. Whitefield.
Lith. of Endicott & Co. N.Y.
New York. Published by E. Whitefield.
Entered . . . 1852 . . .
16½ x 33¾
Collections: MMNN, NYHS, NYPL

58 TAGHANIC FALL. / (215 feet high) / Near Ithaca Tomkins Co. N.Y.
Drawn from Nature by E. Whitefield.
On stone by D. Glasgow.
Printed in cols. by Endicott & Co. N.Y.
Published by E. Whitefield 59 Beekman St. N.Y.
Entered . . . 1854 by E. Whitefield.
Collection: NYPL (two; one in S.P. Avery collection)

59 HAMILTON, CANADA WEST. / From the Mountain.
WHITEFIELD'S ORIGINAL VIEWS OF NORTH AMERICAN CITIES No. 29
Drawn from Nature by E. Whitefield.
Lith. of Endicott & Co. N.Y.
Published by E. Whitefield Hamilton 1854.
Entered . . . 1854 by E. Whitefield . . . New York.
[10 references below image]
19⅞ x 35¼
Collections: PAC, ROM

60 TORONTO, CANADA WEST. / From the Top of the Jail.
WHITEFIELD'S ORIGINAL VIEWS OF NORTH AMERICAN CITIES No. 30
Drawn from Nature by E. Whitefield.
Lith. of Endicott & Co. N.Y.
Published by E. Whitefield, Toronto, 1854.
Entered . . . 1854 by E. Whitefield . . . New York.
19 x 35⅝
Collections: Musée Chateau de Ramezay, MMNN, McCord Museum,
    PAC, ROM

61 MONTREAL, CANADA EAST. / From the Mountain, [2nd edition;
        same lettering, with two additions, but a different stone for the image]
WHITEFIELD'S ORIGINAL VIEWS OF NORTH AMERICAN CITIES, No. 25
Drawn from Nature by E. Whitefield.
Lith. of Endicott & Co. N.Y.
Montreal. Published by E. Whitefield, Gt. St. James St.
Entered . . . 1852 by E. Whitefield . . . New York.
[date depicted: 1855]
[20 numbered references below image]
19¼ x 34½
Collections: Musée Chateau de Ramezay, McCord Museum, MMNN,
    PAC, Musée du Quebec, NYPL, ROM
    ROM also owns a proof before letters.

62 QUEBEC. / FROM BEAUPORT.
WHITEFIELD'S VIEWS OF NORTH AMERICAN CITIES No. 31
Drawn from Nature & on Stone by E. Whitefield.
Printed in tint by Maclear & Co. Toronto, C.W.
Published by E. Whitefield, 16 King St. Toronto.
Entered . . . 1855
19⅛ x 33⅝
Collections: MMNN, PAC

63 [BRANTFORD, CANADA WEST?]
[WHITEFIELD'S ORIGINAL VIEWS OF NORTH AMERICAN CITIES No. 32]

64 KINGSTON, CANADA WEST. / From Fort Henry.
WHITEFIELD'S ORIGINAL VIEWS OF NORTH AMERICAN CITIES No. 33
Drawn from Nature by E. Whitefield.
Kingston. Published by E. Whitefield, 1855.
Copyright Secured.
[11 references below image]
19¾ x 34½
Collections: Musée Chateau de Ramezay, PAC, ROM

65 OTTAWA CITY, CANADA WEST / (Late Bytown.)
WHITEFIELD'S ORIGINAL VIEWS OF NORTH AMERICAN CITIES No. 34
View of the Uppertown, looking up the Ottawa River from Government Hill.
Drawn from Nature by E. Whitefield.
Ottawa. Published by E. Whitefield, 1855.
[5 references below image]
19¾ x 36
Collections: NYPL, PAC, ROM

66 OTTAWA CITY, CANADA WEST / Lower Town.
WHITEFIELD'S ORIGINAL VIEWS OF NORTH AMERICAN CITIES No. 35
From Government Hill looking down the Ottawa River and showing the locks of the Rideau Canal.
Drawn from Nature by E. Whitefield.
Ottawa. Published by E. Whitefield, 1855.
19¾ x 36
Collections: McCord Museum, PAC, ROM

67 LONDON, CANADA WEST
WHITEFIELD'S ORIGINAL VIEWS OF NORTH AMERICAN CITIES No. 36
Drawn from Nature by E. Whitefield.
London. Published by E. Whitefield, 1855.
Entered . . . 1855 . . .
[11 references below image]
19¼ x 35⅛
Collections: London Public Library and Art Museum, NYPL, PAC, ROM

68 VIEW OF GALENA, ILL.
WHITEFIELD'S ORIGINAL VIEWS OF NORTH AMERICAN CITIES No. 37

Drawn from Nature by E. Whitefield.
Lith. of Endicott & Co. N.Y.
Galena, published by E. Whitefield, 1856.
Entered . . . 1856 by E. Whitefield . . . Illinois.
[10 numbered references below image]
19½ x 36
Collections: CHS, Missouri Historical Society, St. Louis, NYPL

69 VIEW OF NIAGARA FALLS
WHITEFIELD'S ORIGINAL VIEWS OF NORTH AMERICAN SCENERY, No. 38
Drawn from Nature by E. Whitefield.
Lith. of Endicott & Co., N.Y.
Entered . . . by E. Whitefield [no date] . . .
[probably 1856]
19¼ x 35½
Collection: PAC

70 VIEW OF ST. ANTHONY, MINNEAPOLIS, AND ST. ANTHONY'S FALLS. / From Cheever's Tower. 1857.
WHITEFIELD'S ORIGINAL VIEWS OF NORTH AMERICAN CITIES, No. 39
Published by E. Whitefield.
Drawn from Nature by E. Whitefield.
Lith. of Endicott & Co. N.Y.
Entered . . . 1857 by E. Whitefield . . . Minnesota Ter.y.
[9 references below image.]
24 x 36
Collections: MHS, NYPL

Minnesota Scenery

71 EXPLORING PARTY IN MINNESOTA
Encampment on Fairy Lake July 1857.
From Nature by E. Whitefield.
J. Gemmell Lith, 132 Lake St. Chicago.
[On stone:] E. Whitefield.
Published by Rufus Blanchard Chicago Ill.
[1858]
10¼ x 14¼
Collection: BPL

72 KANDOTTA, M. T.
Fairy Lake in the Distance.
Drawn by E. Whitefield.
Lith. by J. Gemmell 132 Lake St. Chicago.
[1858]
10¼ x 14¾
Collection: MHS

73 MINNEHAHA
WHITEFIELD'S SERIES OF MINNESOTA SCENERY, No. 3
From Nature by E. Whitefield.
Gemmell Lith. 132 Lake St. Chicago.
[On stone:] E. Whitefield.
Entered . . . 1858 by E. Whitefield & Rufus Blanchard . . .
14¼ x 10⅛
Collections: BPL, MHS
Note: This lithograph was also the center illustration for a broadside
entitled "Minnesota Land Agency. E. Whitefield Dealer in Real
Estate, St. Paul, M.T." published by Rufus Blanchard in 1857.

74 MINNEHAHA
WHITEFIELD'S SERIES OF MINNESOTA SCENERY, No. 4
From Nature by E. Whitefield.
J. Gemmell Lith. 132 Lake St. Chicago.
Published by Rufus Blanchard Chicago Ill.
Entered . . . 1858 by E. Whitefield and Rufus Blanchard . . .
[On stone:] E. Whitefield.
14½ x 10¼
Collection: BPL

Note: The following lithograph is given here in proper chronological
order but is part of the Chicago series beginning with view number 84.

75 VIEW OF ILLINOIS AND MICHIGAN CENTRAL DEPOT &C.
WHITEFIELD'S VIEWS OF CHICAGO
From the Corner of Madison St. and Michigan Avenue.
From Nature by E. Whitefield.
Lith. & Printed by CHAS. SHOBER 109 Lake St. Chicago.
Published by E. Whitefield at D. B. Cooke & Cos. Lake St. Chicago.
Entered . . . 1860 by E. Whitefield . . .

10¾ x 18⅛, tinted
Collections: CHS, EI

WHITEFIELD'S PATENT COMBINATION DRAWING CARDS. / First Series. /
Views on the Upper Mississippi.
Note: The Patented Drawing Cards were offered for sale, according to
diary references, in 1861. Although the Mississippi series was the only
one published, Whitefield began work on others. The Gardiner collection contains two Hudson River scenes on wood panels; the Gardiners
also own three pencil and wash drawings on bristol board that portray
landscape scenes of the ruins of a Gothic church, a sixteenth-century
castle, and a view on the Rhine. The Boston Public Library owns two
other cards. Each series is composed of interconnecting scenes.

The Mississippi Series:
76 *Bluff at Red Wing, Minn.*
77 *Near Wabashaw, Minn.*
78 *Approach to Winona, Minn.*
79 *Near Homer, Minn.*
80 *Near Brownsville, Minn.*
81 *Bluff below Lansing, Iowa.*
82 *Near Trempeleau, Wisc.*
83 *From Davenport, Iowa.*
Each 8½ x 5½
Collection: CHS

Views of Chicago

84 VIEW OF CLARK & WELLS ST. BRIDGES
E. WHITEFIELDS VIEWS OF CHICAGO
From the Foot of River St.
From Nature by E. Whitefield.
Lith. & Printed by CHAS. SHOBER 109 Lake St. Chicago.
Publ. by E. Whitefield at D. B. Cooke & Cos. Lake St. Chicago.
Entered . . . 1861 by E. Whitefield . . .
10⅝ x 18³⁄₁₆, tinted
Collections: CHS, EI

85 VIEW OF MICHIGAN AVE., &c. / From Sturges & Buckingham's Elevator
E. WHITEFIELDS VIEWS OF CHICAGO
From Nature by E. Whitefield.
Lith. & print. CHAS. SHOBER 109 Lake St. Chicago.
Published by E. Whitefield at Rufus Blanchard, 52 La Salle St. Chicago.
Entered . . . by E. Whitefield, 1861 . . .
10⁹⁄16 x 18½, tinted
Collections: CHS, EI, MMNN

86 VIEW OF SHERMAN HOUSE / COURT HOUSE &c. / Looking up Randolph
St.
WHITEFIELDS VIEWS OF CHICAGO
From Nature by E. Whitefield.
Lith. print. by CHAS. SHOBER 109 Lake St. Chicago.
Published by E. Whitefield at Rufus Blanchard 52 La Salle St. Chicago.
Entered . . . 1861 . . .
10¾ x 18⅜, tinted
Collections: CHS, EI

87 VIEW OF RUSH ST. BRIDGE &c.
E. WHITEFIELDS VIEWS OF CHICAGO
From Nortons Block River St.
From Nature by E. Whitefield.
Lith. & Printed by CHAS. SHOBER 109 Lake St. Chicago.
Publ. by E. Whitefield at Rufus Blanchard's 52 La Salle St. Chicago.
Entered . . . 1861 by E. Whitefield . . .
10½ x 18, tinted
Collections: CHS, EI, MMNN

88 VIEW OF THE TREMONT HOUSE NC. / (Corner of Dearborn & Lake Sts.)
WHITEFIELD'S VIEWS OF CHICAGO
Looking down Lake Street.
From Nature by E. Whitefield.
Lith. & print. by CHAS. SHOBER 109 Lake St. Chicago.
Publ. by E. Whitefield at Rufus Blanchard 52 La Salle St. Chicago.
Entered . . . 1861 . . .
10¾ x 18¼, tinted
Collections: CHS, EI

89 MICHIGAN TERRACE, / MICHIGAN AVENUE. / Looking towards the
Central Depot.
WHITEFIELDS VIEWS OF CHICAGO

From Nature by E. Whitefield.
Lith. & printed by CHAS. SHOBER Chicago.
Published by E. Whitefield 52 La Salle St. Chicago.
Entered . . . 1863, by E. Whitefield . . .
Owned and occupied by [11 names]
10½ x 17⅞, tinted
Collections: BPL, CHS, EI

Later City Views

90 VIEW OF THE PUBLIC GARDEN & BOSTON COMMON.
From Arlington St.
From Nature by E. Whitefield.
J. H. Bufford's Lith.
Published by P. R. Stewart & Co.
Entered . . . 1866 by E. Whitefield . . .
15¼ x 28½
Collections: BA, BPL, CHS, Library of Congress, SSTB
Original watercolors in Boston Athenaeum (14½ x 28½) and
Boston Museum of Fine Arts (14 x 28½ watermark: Whatman 1873).

91 [VIEW OF FITCHBURG, MASS.]
[Proof before letters]
[Signed on stone:] E. Whitefield.
[c. 1866]
19⅞ x 35½
Collection: Mrs. Bigelow Crocker, Fitchburg, Mass.
Original watercolor in Fitchburg Art Museum, 19 x 35¼ (sight).

92 VIEW OF PORTSMOUTH, N.H. / On July 4th, 1873.
From the head of the North Pond.
Drawn from Nature, by E. Whitefield.
Entered . . . 1873 by E. Whitefield . . .
12 x 22¼ (sepia photoreproduction of the drawing)
Collections: Library of Congress, Strawbery Banke

93 VIEW OF PORTSMOUTH, N.H. / On July 4th, 1873.
From the head of Mt. Vernon Street, looking across the South Mill-Pond.
Drawn from Nature, by E. Whitefield.
Entered . . . 1873, by E. Whitefield . . .

12 x 22¼ (sepia photoreproduction of the drawing)
Collections: EI (right half only—the backing for a Whitefield watercolor), Strawbery Banke, Library of Congress.
Original watercolor in Boston Museum of Fine Arts, 15½ x 30¼.

94 MALDEN, MASS.
Sketched from Nature by E. Whitefield.
Entered . . . 1875, by E. Whitefield . . .
15⅞ x 21⅜ (sepia photoreproduction of the drawing)
Collectons: BPL, Malden Public Library
Original watercolor in the Boston Museum of Fine Arts, 25 x 38.

95 NEWBURYPORT, MASS. in the year 1876. / From Belleville Church.
Drawn from Nature by E. Whitefield in 1876.
Entered . . . 1876.
13 x 20⅜ (sepia photoreproduction of the drawing)
Collections: BA, AAS

96 VIEW OF WORCESTER, MASS. / From Worcester Academy, Union Hill.
Drawn from Nature, by Whitefield in 1876.
Entered . . . 1876 . . .
12½ x 20¼ (sepia photoreproduction of the drawing)
Collection: AAS
Original watercolor in the Worcester (Mass.) Art Museum, 25½ x 39⅜.

97 VIEW OF LOWELL, MASS. / From Centerville.
Drawn from Nature, by E. Whitefield, 1876.
11⅛ x 20 (sepia photoreproduction of the drawing)
Collections: Mrs. Frances Bond, Wellesley, Mass.; ROM, which also owns the original watercolor, 32¼ x 55¾.

98 THE HOME OF WHITTIER / Including the Villages of Amesbury and Salisbury, with Newburyport in the Distance. / From Powwow Hill.
[No copy of this view, evidently another photoreproduction, has yet been found. There is a printed card in the Whitefield collection at the Boston Public Library that reads:

Testimonial,
E. WHITEFIELD,   Amesbury, 9th Mo., 1876
    Dear Friend,
        I have carefully looked over thy picture of our Village and the Valleys of the Merrimac and Powow; and am glad to find it a very excellent representation of one of the finest views in the State.
                                            JOHN G. WHITTIER

And on the reverse:
    It is from a highly finished India ink drawing taken on the spot by E. Whitefield, and is mounted on heavy bristol board, 22 x 28 inches, including margin, price $5. . . . A smaller edition, similar in every respect, excepting in size, $1.50.]

99 VIEW OF DEDHAM, MASS. in 1876.
[On stone:] Drawn from Nature by E. Whitefield.
Entered . . . 1877 . . .
16½ x 26¼ (sepia photoreproduction of the drawing)
Collections: AAS, BPL, Dedham Historical Society, which also owns the original drawing, 19⅞ x 31¾.

100 QUINCY, MASS.
[On stone:] From Nature, by E. Whitefield, 1877.
Entered . . . 1878 . . .
[13 references below image]
16⅞ x 32¼
Collections: BPL, Massachusetts Historical Society

MISCELLANEOUS SINGLE LITHOGRAPHS

101 WRECK OF THE SWALLOW [1845]
The only correct View.
As seen on the morning after the disaster April 7th 1845.
From an Original Drawing taken on the Athens shore (Hudson in the Distance).
Lith. by Lewis & Brown, 37 John St., N.Y.
7½ x 14
Collection: MMNN

102 TOWNSEND'S FURNACE AND MACHINE SHOP [c. 1845]
Corner of Hawk and Elk Sts. Albany
Franklin Townsend & Co.
Manufacturers of Steam-Engines, [boilers], machinery, and all kinds of castings.
Drawn from Nature and on stone by E. Whitefield.
15⅜ x 21⅛
Collection: Avis and Rockwell Gardiner, Stamford, Conn.

103 [Eaton's Coach Factory, Atlantic Dock, 1846]
[Diary reference only.]

104 [Lunatic Hospital at Williamsburg, Va., 1846]
[For Michelin. Diary reference only.]

105 [Ransom's Foundry, 1846]
[Also portrayed in *View of Albany, N.Y.* Diary reference only.]

106 [Albany Iron Works, 1846]
[Diary reference only.]

107 [Winslow's Iron Works, 1846]
[Diary reference, which also mentions Van Norden as printer.]

108 POTTER'S MEETING HOUSE. GOOD LUCK, N.J. [1846]
Drawn by E. Whitefield.
4 x 8
Collection: Historical Society of Pennsylvania

109 [Factory c. 1846]
From Nature by E. Whitefield.
Lith. of Michelin, III, Nassau St.
9⅝ x 3⅜
Collection: Avis and Rockwell Gardiner (proof)

110 A SOUTH-EAST VIEW OF YE GREAT TOWN OF BOSTON IN NEW ENGLAND IN AMERICA
Published for E. Whitefield by A. Tompkins, 38 Cornhill, Boston, in 1848.
[Lithograph facsimile, on a slightly reduced scale, of the Price-Burgis engraving of 1743. Commissioned by Josiah Quincy. Reproduced again on a smaller scale by the albertype process.]
Collections: BA, BPL, Bostonian Society (Old State House, Boston), Massachusetts Historical Society, SSTB

111 [Bush & Lobdell's Foundry, 1850]
[In Wilmington, Del. Diary reference only.]

112 [Belcher's Sugar Refinery, St. Louis, 1859]
[Diary reference only.]

113 [Capt. Brown's Steamboat, St. Louis, 1859]
[Diary reference. Whitefield also mentioned executing drawings of Montreal boats for MacPherson, Crane & Co. in 1852; no steamboat cards attributable to Whitefield have yet been found.]

114 THE REPUBLICAN STANDARD
[A broadside with a center illustration of Candidate for the Presidency Abraham Lincoln poling a flat boat on the Mississippi River, with Quincy, Illinois, in the background. Republican Wigwam at lower left. Capitol at Washington at lower right. With text.]
[Below portrait of Lincoln:]
From Nature by E. Whitefield 1860.
Drawn and engraved on wood by F. H. Brown, Chicago.
Pool & Dean, Printers.
Published by Rufus Blanchard, Chicago.
Broadside, 28 x 23
View of Lincoln, 7 x 11
Collection: Minnesota Historical Society

115 REPUBLICAN WIGWAM
Erected by the Republicans of Chicago for the Campaign of 1860, capable of holding 10,000 persons.
Published by McNally & Co. Booksellers & Newsdealers 81 Dearborn St.
Sketched by E. Whitefield.
6¾ x 11⅛
Collections: Rockwell and Avis Gardiner (proof), CHS, Mr. and Mrs. John M. Norton

116 RISTORI YOKE [1867]
[Copyright, Library of Congress]

Note: Many of the individual lithographs for the series, *Homes of our Forefathers*, especially of more noted houses, were copyrighted individually by Whitefield, from 1886 to 1892.
There are miscellaneous chromolithographed landscape views, executed in the 1870's and 1880's, which fall into at least three groups
1. *Whitefield's Canadian Views*, 8 known, all approx. 4½ x 7.
2. [untitled] 5 river views, approx. 3 x 5.
3. One river view, 6½ x 9.

4 *Illustrations in Books and Magazines*

The most important books in which illustrations by Whitefield appear are *American Wildflowers In Their Native Haunts* and the series *Homes of our Forefathers*. For these, lists of illustrations follow. All other known books and magazines with Whitefield illustrations are listed at the end of this section.

American Wildflowers In Their Native Haunts, or, *Nature's Gems.*
  Emma C. Embury.
  New York: D. Appleton; and Philadelphia: G. Appleton & Company, 1845.
  Frontispiece.—Falling Spring and Dial Mountain, at the head of Wyoming Valley, Pa.
  The Wild Honeysuckle.—Fall on Buttermilk Creek, Pa.
  Fairy Flax, and Crow-Foot Geranium.—Passaic Falls, New Jersey.
  Bellwort.—View near the city of Hudson, New York,
  Early Asclepias.—Otsego Lake, New York,
  Wild Columbine.—Matanga Fall, Pennsylvania,
  Slender-leaved Gerardia.—View near Fort Montgomery,
  Blue-Eyed Grass.—View on the Hudson, near Verplanck's Point,
  Broad-Leaved Laurel.—Yantic Falls, Norwich, Conn,
  Prince's Pine.—View near Poughkeepsie,
  Adder's Tongue Violet.—View near Tioga Point, Pennsylvania,
  Hare-Bell and Lespedeza.—Upper Entrance of the Highlands,
  The Wild Rose.—View on Staten Island,
  Brook-Lime.—Distant View of Albany,
  Eye Bright.—View from Constitution Island, opposite West Point,
  Wild Strawberry.—Distant View of Cattawissa, Pennsylvania,
  Azure Star Flower.—View on the Susquehanna, near Nineveh,
  Cardinal Flower.—Outlet of Fishkill Creek,
  Yellow Star Grass.—View on the Juniata, Pennsylvania,
  Wood Lily.—High Bridge and Croton Fountain at Haarlem, N.Y.

The Homes of our Forefathers, being a collection of the Oldest and Most Interesting Buildings in Massachusetts.
  From Original Drawings, by E. Whitefield.
  With Historical Memoranda.
  Boston: Published by A. Williams & Co., 283 Washington Street.
  Subscription copy. 1879. Copyright by E. Whitefield 1879.

Note: Oblong octavo, green or maroon cloth cover with gold Gothic lettering. All lettering is by hand on the stone; the town name, in Gothic script, is centered above the picture, the house name, below. As many as forty-two views were drawn on one stone, and cut later. Almost all the drawings have "E.W." on the stone; the Longfellow House has "E. Whitefield, 1879." Two tints are used; most views have a tint border line. In the following list, and in succeeding lists, original sketches, wash drawings, or finished pencil drawings at the Boston Public Library are indicated by •, those at the Society for the Preservation of New England Antiquities by ×.

	Cambridge	The Longfellow House
•	× Concord	The Hubbard House
	× Dedham	The Fairbanks House /1636/ oldest in Mass.
	× Duxbury	The Standish House
•	× Melrose	The Lynde House
	× Revere	The Floyd House
	Kingston	The Bradford House
•	Ipswich	The Bond House
•	Andover	The Holt House
•	Brookline	The Aspinwall House
•	West Roxbury	The Curtis House
	× Quincy	The Adams Houses
	× Hingham	The Old Meeting House
•	× Medford	The Cradock [Craddock] House
•	× Newbury	The Poor House
	× Rockport	The Gott House
	× Swampscott	The Mudge Farm House
	× Marblehead	St. Michael's Church
•	Salem	The Prince House
•	Wenham	The Ober House
	× Newbury	The Noyes House
	Plymouth	The Bradford House
	[Boston]	The Old North [Church]
•	[Boston]	The Old South [Church]
	× Lowell	The Dracut Garrison House
•	× Saugus	The Old Iron Works House
	× Concord	The Old Manse
	Lexington	The Tidd House
	× Lynn	The Lewis House
	× Newburyport	The Pillsbury House
	Pembroke	The Barker House—The oldest house in N. England!

Wakefield	The Hartshorne House
• × Gloucester	The White or Ellery House
Peabody	The Buxton House
Newbury	The Little House
× Duxbury	The Alden House
• Rowley	The Clark House
• Watertown	The Brown House
• Beverly	The Baker House
• × Salem	The Palmer House
Brookline	The Gardner House
• Arlington	The Teel House
Cambridge	The Wadsworth House
• Cambridge	The Holmes House
Reading	The Sweetzer House
• North Andover	The Bradstreet House
Marblehead	The Moll Pitcher House
• Hingham	The Folsom House
Milton	The Vose House
Dorchester	The Pierce House
Kingston	The Cushman House
× Kingston	The Willett House
• Concord	The Alcott House
• × Revere	The Yeaman House

The Homes of our Forefathers, being a selection of the Oldest and Most Interesting Buildings in Massachusetts. [Second edition]
From Original Drawings, by E. Whitefield.
With Historical Memoranda.
Boston: Published by A. Williams & Co., 283 Washington Street.
Subscription copy. 1879. Copyright by E. Whitefield.

Note: There is no "second edition" so named, but there are some copies which are slightly different from the first edition but not labeled "third." The change is primarily the inconsistent substitution of eight to ten drawings of houses. The order of the approximately forty-five illustrations in common is different in every copy examined. Other changes are the substitution of the word "collection" for "selection" on the title-page, block letters for Gothic script on the cover, and the addition, in some copies, of a quote by Thomas Amory after the title-page. The copy at Harvard is dated 1880, but retains the words "subscription copy."

Illustrations new with various "second editions":

× Haverhill	Birthplace of John Whittier
× Haverhill	Saltonstall House
× Danvers	The Endicott or Nourse House
• Ipswich	Saltonstall House
× Newbury	The Coffin House
• × Cohasset	The Lincoln House
Cohasset	The Nichols House
Stoneham	The Old Parsonage House
Kingston	The Allerton or Cobb House

The Homes of our Forefathers, being a selection of the Oldest and Most Interesting Buildings, Historical Houses, and Noted Places in Massachusetts.

From Original Drawings made on the Spot by Edwin Whitefield.
Third Edition.
Copyrighted by Edwin Whitefield, 1880.
Boston: A. Williams and Company, 283 Washington Street, 1880.

Note: Twenty-three plates are in all three editions. The stones are the same, but the lettering is changed in this edition: the town name appears below the picture, after the house name. For ease of reference, however, the list below gives town name first, as above. Again, this appears to be a non-standard edition.

Illustrations new with the various third editions:

• Sudbury	The Wayside Inn
Newton	The Hammond House
× Lexington	The Munroe House
Woburn	The Cutler House
× Woburn	The Rumford House
• Everett	The Edmester House
Wilmington	The Carter House
• Billerica	The Danforth House
North Reading	The Batchelder House
Swampscott	The Humphrey House
Danvers	The Peabody House
Lynn	The Moulton House
North Andover	The Abbott House
Ipswich	The Sutton House
Dorchester	The Wells Mansion
× Danvers	The Jacobs House

Danvers	The Fowler House
Danvers	Gen¹ Putnam's Birthplace
Salem	The Roger Williams House
Salem	The Narbonne House
Salem	The Turner House
• × Salem	The Old Bakery
• Byfield	The Longfellow House
• Byfield	The Dummer Mansion
• Gloucester	The Dennison and Chard Houses
• × Saugus	The Boardman House
Leicester	Woodland Site
• Newburyport	The Toppan House

Six unidentified houses in Manchester-by-the-sea, Boston, Reading, Groveland, South Scituate, Scituate.

The Homes of our Forefathers, being a selection of the Oldest and Most Interesting Buildings, Historical Houses, and Noted Places in Rhode Island and Connecticut.[26]

From Original Drawings made on the Spot by Edwin Whitefield.
Boston: Whitefield and Crocker, 25 Bromfield Street, 1882.

× The Bull House, Newport, R.I.
× The Atkinson House, Newport, R.I.
× The Bishop Berkley House, Newport, R.I.
× Channing's Birth-place, Newport, R.I.
× The Bosworth House, Bristol, R.I.
× Reynolds House, Bristol, R.I.
× Blackstone's Grave, Lonsdale, R.I.
   The Williams House, Providence, R.I.
× Tillinghast Mansion, Providence, R.I.
   Whipple or Abbott House, Providence, R.I.
× The Phillips Mansion, Wickford, R.I.
× Updike House, Wickford, R.I.
× The Eddy House, Warren, R.I.
   The Hazard House, Kingston, R.I.
× The Paine House, Conanicut, R.I.
× The Carr House, Conanicut, R.I.
× The Caesar House, Providence, R.I.
× Fenner House, Johnston, R.I.
× The Old Ballou Church, Cumberland, R.I.
   Coddington House, Newport, R.I.
× The Governor Greene House, E. Greenwich, R.I.
× King House, Newport, R.I.

× The Whitefield House, Guilford, Conn. [signed and dated, 1881, on stone]
× The Griswold House, Guilford
   The Saltonstall House, Branford, Conn.
× The Roger Sherman House, New Haven
× The Huntington House, Norwich Town
× The Dr. Turner Place, Norwich Town
× The Denison House, Stonington
   The Mortimer Mansion, Middletown, Conn.
× The Boardman House, Rocky Hill, Conn.
× The Rollins House, Rocky Hill
   The Clark or Porter House, Farmington
× The Whitman House, Farmington
   Scovill or Johnson House, Waterbury
   Arnold House, New Haven
   Winthrop Mansion and Mill, New London
   Hempstead House, New London
× The Patterson House, Berlin
× The Beckly House, Berlin
× Deserted Mansion, Vernon
   Old Tavern & Store, Bolton, Conn.
   The Gov. Walcott House, Litchfield
   The Gould House, Litchfield
   The Kingsbury House, Waterbury
   The Adams, or Chapman House, Waterbury
   The Hurlbut House, Winchester
   John Brown's Birthplace, Torrington
   Jackson House, Derby, Conn.
   Old Academy, Derby, Conn.
   Rowley or Lacey House, Bridgeport, Conn.
   Nichols House, Bridgeport, Conn.
   The Clark House, Stratford
   The Judson House, Stratford
   Avery House (No. 1) Groton
   Avery House (No. 2) Groton
× The Webb Mansion, Wethersfield
   The Hollister House, Wethersfield
× The Barnard House, Hartford
   Noah Webster's Birth-place, W. Hartford
× Govr Trumbull's Residence, Lebanon
× Govr Trumbull's War Office, Lebanon
   The Lynes House, Norwalk
   Old House, Norwalk
× The Old Stone Fort, Windsor

Old School-House
Silliman House, Bridgeport
Hobart House, Fairfield
× Judge Swift House, Windham
The Johnson House, Putnam
× The Allyn House, Windsor
× The Moore House, Windsor
The Stowe House, Milford
× Old-Fashioned Country Store, Norwich Town
× Olmstead House, East Hartford
× The Lynde House, Hartford
× The Seymour House, Hartford
× Cluster of Old Houses, Hartford
× Griswold House, Wethersfield
The Butler House, Wethersfield
The Seelye House, Bethel, Conn.
The Lord House, Old Lyme
The Washington House, Stamford, Conn.
The Hotchkiss House, Derby, Conn.
× [Nathan] Hale's Birthplace, Coventry
The Trumbull House, Watertown, Conn.

The Homes of our Forefathers, being a selection of the Oldest and Most Interesting Historical Houses and Noted Places in Maine, New Hampshire, and Vermont.
From Original Drawings Taken on the Spot, by Edwin Whitefield.
Reading, Mass.: E. Whitefield, 1886.

× York, Me.	The McIntire Garrison House
× York, Me.	The Jenkins Garrison House
• × Saco, Me.	Kelley House
× Saco, Me.	The Cutts Mansion
× Kennebunk, Me.	Emerson House
× Kennebunkport, Me.	Walker House
× Saco, Me.	The Cleeve or Cleaves House
× Saco, Me.	Warren House
× Kittery, Me.	The Sparhawk House
• × Kittery, Me.	The Pepperell Mansion
× Gorham, Me.	The McLellan House
× Gorham, Me.	The Old McLellan House
× York, Me.	The Bradbury House
× Hiram, Me.	The Wadsworth House
× Hardings, Me.	The Weston House
× Biddeford, Me.	The Haley House

× Kennebunkport, Me.	The Nevin House
× Harpswell Neck, Me.	The Dunning House
× Bath, Me.	The Sam'l Sewell House
× Bath, Me.	The Sewell House
× Bangor, Me.	The Harlow House
× Saco, Me.	The Old Cutts House and Store
× Orr's Island, Me.	The Orr House
× Biddeford, Me.	The Payson House
× Brewer, Me.	The Holyoke House
× Biddeford, Me.	The Thatcher House
× Portland, Me.	Longfellow's Birth-place
× Portland, Me.	The Wadsworth-Longfellow House
× Brunswick, Me.	The Thompson House
× Biddeford, Me.	The Dean House
× York, Me.	Old Jail
× Gardiner, Me.	Old Post Office
× Castine, Me.	The Tilden House
• × Livermore, Me.	The Livermore House
× Kittery, Me.	The Bray or Underwood House
× Vassalboro, Me.	The Cole House
× Bath, Me.	The Chadbourne House
× Scarboro, Me.	The King House
× Biddeford, Me.	Old Custom House
× Deering, Me.	The Stevens House
× Pittston, Me.	Colburn House
× Pittston, Me.	Stevens House
× Portland, Me.	The Cox House
× Portland, Me.	The McClellan House
× Bath, Me.	The Crocker House
× Bath, Me.	The Webb House
× Augusta, Me.	Fort Western
× Winslow, Me.	Block House
Exeter, N.H.	The Col. Nathaniel Gilman House
Exeter, N.H.	The Governor Gilman House
Exeter, N.H.	Phillips Academy building No. 1
Exeter, N.H.	Phillips Academy No. 2
Laconia, N.H.	The Bradbury House
× Dunbarton, N.H.	The Stewart House
Amherst, N.H.	Horace Greeley's Birth-place
Concord, N.H.	Garrison House
Chesterfield, N.H.	The Marsh House
× Portsmouth, N.H.	The Jackson House

× Newcastle, N.H.	The Yeaton House
Westmoreland, N.H.	Baptist Church
Laconia, N.H.	The Jewett House
× Manchester, N.H.	The Blodgett House
• × Manchester, N.H.	The Stark House
Concord, N.H.	The Eastman House
Nashua, N.H.	The Lovewell House
Nashua, N.H.	The Eayers or Epps House
× Dover, N.H.	The Varney House
× Newcastle, N.H.	The Jaffray House
Concord, N.H.	The Rolfe-Rumford House
Concord, N.H.	The Walker House
Exeter, N.H.	The Leavitt House
Exeter, N.H.	The Folsom House
× Portsmouth, N.H.	The John Moffat House (a photograph; not in the copy at the Boston Athenaeum)
× Little Harbor, N.H.	The Old Wentworth Mansion
× Portsmouth, N.H.	The Vaughn House
Tilton, N.H.	The Tilton Homestead
× Portsmouth, N.H.	The Jaffray House
Exeter, N.H.	The Daniel Gilman House
Exeter, N.H.	The Tilton or King House
Exeter, N.H.	Old Post Office
Exeter, N.H.	The Birthplace of Gen¹ Cass
Keene, N.H.	The Daniels-Seward House
× Keene, N.H.	The Heaton House
× Exeter, N.H.	Daniel Webster's Birthplace
Exeter, N.H.	The Jangrin House
Exeter, N.H.	The Odiorne House
Exeter, N.H.	The Gordon House
Exeter, N.H.	The Hackett-Peabody House
× Dover, N.H.	The Ham House
Salisbury	Daniel Webster's Birthplace
Sanbornton	Colby-Leavitt House
Manchester Center	The Hall House
Manchester Center	The Old Town House
Canterbury	The Clough House
Canterbury	The Gerrish House
Laconia	The Boynton House
Gilford	The Blaisdell House
Bennington, Vt.	The Matthews House
× Bennington, Vt.	The Harwood House

× Brattleboro, Vt.	The Sargeant House
• Ludlow, Vt.	The Whitcomb House
• Rutland, Vt.	The Post House
Brattleboro, Vt.	The Hayes House
• Rutland, Vt.	The Gould House
Vernon, Vt.	The Bridgeman Fort
Montpelier, Vt.	The Cadwell House
Bennington, Vt.	Catamount Tavern
• Rutland, Vt.	The Jenkins House
Bennington, Vt.	The Old Town Poor House

The Homes of our Forefathers in Boston, Old England, and Boston, New England.

[Deluxe Edition]:
From Original Drawings by Edwin Whitefield.
E. Whitefield, 211 Tremont Street. Boston, Mass.
Copyright by Edwin Whitefield 1889.
All rights reserved.
Chromolithographs mounted on bristol board.
Original price, $15.

[Regular Edition]:
From Original Drawings by Edwin Whitefield.
Damrell & Upham, Boston, Mass.
Copyright by Edwin Whitefield 1889.
Chromolithographs on heavy paper.
Original price, $6.

Frontispiece: St. Botolph's Church [Boston, England]

England

• The Church Alms House	• Old House in Stanbow Lane
• Bridge over the Witham	• Hussey Castle
• Barnham-Burton House	• The Old Jerusalem House
• Old Chantry Chapel	• Tomb of a Knight
• Rev. John Cotton's Vicarage	• Tomb of a Lady
• John Foxe's Birthplace	• Old Monastery
• Old Flemish House, Mitre Lane	Rochford Tower
• The Grammar School	St. Botolph's Church
• The Guildhall	Shod Friar's Hall
• Heron's Hall	• The Three Tuns Inn
• Old House on Church Street	• The White Horse Inn
• Ancient House, Archer Lane	

New England

- Aspinwall House, Brookline
- Auchmuty House, Roxbury
- The Badger House, Prince Street
- Blackstone's House
- The Blake House, Dorchester
- Capen House, Union Street
- Christ Church, Salem Street
- The Clough House, Margaret Street
  Clough-Vernon House, Vernon Court
  Craft's House, Tremont St., near Brookline
- The Curtis House
- Edw. Everett's Birth-place, Dorchester
- The Faneuil Mansion
  First Meeting House
- The Galloupe House, Hull St.
- Gardner House, Pleasant St., Dorchester
- The Gray House
- The Green Dragon Inn
- The Hancock Tavern, Corn Court
- The Hartt House, Hull Street
- Kimball-Parker House, Unity Street
  Kings Chapel, Tremont Street
- Orange-Lincoln House, Salem Street
- Mather-Eliot House, Hanover Street
- The Newman House
- The Old Feather Store
- The Ochtorlony House, North Street
  Old Corner Bookstore
  Old State House
- The Old South Church
  The Paul Revere House, North Square
  The Pierce House, Dorchester
- The Province House
- Sheafe House, Essex St.
- Shirley House, Dorchester
  Sun Tavern, as it was originally
  The Thoreau House
- The Tileston House, Prince Street
- The Tremere House, North Street
- The Warren House
- The Wells Mansion, Salem Street

The Homes of our Forefathers in Massachusetts.
  From Original Drawings by Edwin Whitefield.
  New Edition.
  Copyright by Edwin Whitefield, Dedham, Mass. 1892.
  Two versions:
    Chromolithographs pasted on bristol board.
    Black ink lithographs on different colored paper.
  Frontispiece: photo of Whitefield
  Note: Eight of the houses depicted were in all three former editions, although the stones were new to this edition; fourteen others were in one or two former editions. Seventeen (indicated by *) were new to this edition. The Dummer Mansion had become the Dummer Academy. Most of the views have "copyright by E. Whitefield 1892."

  Longfellow House, Cambridge
× Whittier's Birth-place, Haverhill
- Holmes House, Cambridge
× The Fairbanks House, Dedham
- The Saltonstall House, Ipswich
  The Wayside Inn, Sudbury
• × Pillsbury House, Newburyport
- Old Shot Tower, Somerville *
• × The Craddock House, Medford
× The Rumford House, Woburn
  Waitt House, Malden *
× The Osgood House, Salisbury *
× Old Stone Bridge, Ipswich *
- The Old Longfellow House, Byfield
× St. Michael's Church, Marblehead
× Conant House, Beverly *
× The Standish House, Duxbury
  The Hovey House, Ipswich, Mass. *
  Chipman House, Nth Beverly *
- Fletcher House, Billerica *
• × Rev. George Whitefield died here. Newburyport *
• × Dodge House, Ipswich *
• × Clark House, Medfield *
  Allerton or Cobb House, Kingston
× Otis House, Scituate *
  Sutton House, Ipswich
× Winthrop House, Ipswich *
- Dummer Academy, Byfield
  Tucker House, Marblehead *

- × Iron Works House, Saugus
  × The Coffin House, Newbury
- × Lynde House, Melrose
  · Barnard House, Amesbury*
  Barker House, Pembroke, 1628
  × The Wood House, New Bedford*
- × White or Ellery House, Gloucester
  The Cutler House, Woburn
  Govr Bradford's House, Plymouth
  × The Burton House, Plymouth*

Other books and magazines containing Whitefield illustrations:

Floral Album. New York: J. C. Riker, 1841.
Sargent's New Monthly Magazine. Volume I. New York: Sargent & Company, 1843.
Illustrated Botany. Volume I, Nos. V, VI, VII, VIII. New York: J. K. Wellman, 1846.
The Juvenile Forget-Me-Not. New York: [?] & Leavitt & Allen, n.d.
The American Flora, or History of Plants and Wild Flowers. A. B. Strong, M.D. 4 volumes. New York: Green & Spencer, 1849–51.

5 *Other Publications and Manuscripts*

DRAWING BOOKS

Instructions in Map Drawing, Illustrated with Colored Plates, being a Complete Guide to That Useful Art. Chicago, 1863.
New England Drawing Books. Landscape Series. Nos. 1–6. Published by Whitefield & Crocker, 15 Bromfield Street, Boston, Mass., 1866.

MAPS

Whitefield's New Map of the Principal Portion of Chicago. Patent applied for by E. Whitefield. J. W. Dean, Printer, 148 Lake St., Chicago, 1864.
Patent Topographical Business Directory, Montreal, C.E. 1864.
Whitefield's New Map of Buffalo, N.Y. Entered ... 1865 by E. Whitefield ... in the northern District of New York.

Courtesy Print Department, Boston Public Library.

NEWS ARTICLES

The Illustrated London News. Jan. 12, 1856.
  "View of Hamilton, in Canada West." Illus: Hamilton.
St. Paul Minnesotian. Sept. 30, Oct. 1, 1856.
Paris Star (Canada West). April, 1857.
  "The Lands of the Ill. Central R. Road Compared with the U. States Lands in Minnesota." "E.W. Mar. 1857"
Leslie's Illustrated News
  "The Territory of Minnesota. The Character of the Country.—How to go West.—Description of St. Anthony and the Falls." Illus: "The Falls and Town of St. Anthony on the upper Miss., over two thousand miles from the Gulf of Mexico, at the head of navigation on the Great Father of Waters. By E. Whitefield, of Minnesota."   May 9, 1857
  "A Trip From St. Anthony to Lake Minnetonka, and Shakopee Lakes, Minnesota Territory." Illus: "Setting out on an Exploring Expedition," "The Claim Shanty," "Emigrant Train Crossing the Prairies," "Catching a Pickerel in Minnetonka Lake," "A Sioux Encampment, on the Banks of the Minnesota River," "View in the Valley of the River Minnesota, A Short Distance from St. Anthony's Falls, Minnesota Territory. From Nature, by E. Whitefield," "Lake Minnetonka, Near St. Anthony's Falls, Minnesota Territory."   May 30, 1857

"A Trip From St. Anthony to the Country around Kandiyohi, Minitaga and Owapi Lakes, Minnesota Territory." Illus: "View on the Upper Mississippi, looking Down From St. Anthony's Falls. From Nature by E. Whitefield.", "The Lake Owapi, A Sioux name meaning picture. From Nature by E. Whitefield.", "View From Kandiyohi, looking down Lakes Minitaga and Kazota. From Nature by E. Whitefield," "Minitaga Lake, as seen from Kandiyohi. From Nature by E. Whitefield." June 3, 1857

Chicago Press and Tribune. May 4, 1859.
   "A Winter Trip to Fort Abercrombie, St. Paul to the Red River of the North. April 12, 1859."
   "From the Mississippi to the Red River of the North." St. Paul, April 26, 1859.

Western Railroad Gazette. C-I. RR. Sept. 19, 1863.
   "Chicago to Cincinnati, via Chicago & Cincinnati Air Line; Towns and Cities along the Route, &c. E. W. Sept. 11, 1863."

The Illustrated London News. July 23, 1864, p. 103.
   "The Great Disaster on the Grand Trunk Railway of Canada." Illus: "Scene of the Disaster at Beloeil Bridge, near Montreal, on the Grand Trunk Railway of Canada."

Boston Traveler. July 22, 1890.
   "Old Boston. Romance of Its Earliest History." Illus: Hancock House— Wells House— 1st Meeting House—Thoreau House (Prince St.)—Tileston House—Gray House.

Boston Globe. 1890. [proposed.]
   A letter from Chas. H. Taylor, Jr., agreeing to take six articles on the labouring classes in England, with sketches with each article. Price to be paid: $125. (Collection BPL).

CIRCULARS

Opinions of the Press. Nicholson, McIntosh & Co's Alligator Press James Street, Hamilton. 1854.

Perspective Drawing and Sketching from Nature. [Hamilton, Canada West, 1854?] (2 versions).

To the Inhabitants of Canada. Hamilton, 1854.

Minnesota Land Agency. E. Whitefield, Dealer in Real Estate, St. Paul, M. T. Entered . . . 1857 by E. Whitefield . . . in the District Court of Massachusetts.

Lecture on Minnesota, Illustrated with a great variety of Paintings. Printed in Dubuque, c. 1857.

Opinions of the Press. Printed in Minnesota, c. 1857.

Whitefield's Patent Combination Drawing Cards. First Series. Views on the Upper Mississippi. Published in Chicago in 1861.

Notosericum. A Novelty in Art. (A Substitute for Embroidery). Boston, 1867.

Just Published. Homes of our Forefathers. 1881.

Just Published. Homes of our Forefathers. c. 1882.

Growth of Cities in the U.S. From the First Census 1790 to 1890 Inclusive . . . Copyright 1891.

JOURNALS

Many manuscript pages in various collections throughout the country were intended for eventual publication. Most complete was "Trip on the N.Y. & Erie R.R. &c &c in the Summer of 1854 [1853]." This journal of 82 pages was meant to accompany the sketches in the sketchbook now owned by the Boston Museum of Fine Arts. Others are the accounts of his exploring trips, "Kandiyohi," "Kandotta," etc., contained in bits and pieces in the collections of the Boston Public Library and the Gardiners. Others still are "Trip to the Sault," "Trip from Chicago to Galena, New Towns on the Miss.," 1855; "Minnesota and Sauk River Valley," and "Minnesota Lakes," both owned by the Minnesota Historical Society; "Quincy to Dunleith," "Cincinnati to Chicago," "Trip to England and Scotland," "Boston, England," and many others, from a few comments to several pages.

6 Derivative Prints

Some of Whitefield's lithographs of Canadian cities were reissued a decade later by Charles Magnus & Cie., in small folio steel engravings. There were two sets, one of the unembellished engraving, the other with a thin gold border surrounded by a printed black mat, treated to resemble high-gloss varnish. There is yet another version of the views of Ottawa and Montreal in photolithograph, hand-colored. The plain steel engraving of Ottawa has an addition in the sky: "Prof. Lowe's first Balloon Ascension / July 17th, 1858." A Magnus view of Ottawa in the Avis and Rockwell Gardiner collection has "From Nature, by E. Whitefield" written on the picture, in Whitefield's hand. The others can be seen in the Public Archives of Canada.

Nineteenth-century book publishers frequently borrowed illustrations, had them engraved, and gave no credit to the original. Consequently, a list of these would take years to compile.

Notes on the Text

1. *American Historical Prints, Early Views of American Cities, &c.* by I. N. Phelps Stokes and Daniel C. Haskell, New York Public Library, 1932. *America on Stone,* Harry T. Peters, New York, 1931.

2. Diaries at the Boston Public Library cover the following periods:
   1842
   1843 (one week in "Po'keepsie & Hudson")
   1846
   1848 (to Mar. 25)
   1850
   1852 (contains 1853)
   "Trip on the N.Y. & Erie R.R. &c &c in the Summer of 1854 [1853]"
   1855 (contains 1856) Also *Stewart's Register.* 1856.
   1858 Diary and "Kandotta," No. 3–Oct. 18 to Dec. 31st, 1858
   1859–1860. "Kandotta," No. 4, Jany. 1st–Dec. 31, 1859.
   1861 (June 7–Aug. 30), and "Chicago Mem–1861."
   1863–1864. "Chicago to Cincinn. Sep. 1863," and "Chicago to Detroit & Montreal, 1864."
   1866 (June through Sept.)
   1882–1883. "Oct. 1882," and Mem^a Cesnola Collec^n (Oct. 31–June)
   1888 "Trip to England." (2 books)
   1889 "Notices of My Books, &c."
   1890 "Trip to R.I. & Conn."; "Trip to N.H., Vt., & Canada."

3. Twenty-two entries to this effect are in an 1840 account book in the Whitefield collection at the Boston Public Library.

4. *American Wildflowers In Their Native Haunts* was published in New York and Philadelphia by D. and G. Appleton & Company, 1845. *The American Flora, or History of Plants and Wild Flowers* by A. B. Strong, M.D., 4 vols.: New-York; 1849–1851, published by Green & Spencer. The Boston Public Library owns the original watercolor for the frontispiece for the Embury book, entitled in this edition *Nature's Gems. Illustrated Botany* was published by J. K. Wellman, 118 Nassau St., New York, 1846. *Sargent's New Monthly Magazine, of Literature, Fashion, and the Fine Arts,* edited by Epes Sargent, New York: Sargent & Company, vol. 1, 1843. The Embury and Strong books courtesy the Massachusetts Horticultural Society, Boston, Mass.; the others courtesy the American Antiquarian Society, Worcester, Mass., which also owns the *Floral Album* of J. C. Riker, New York, 1841,

with five flower lithographs by Whitefield. The Embury book was republished in pocket book form by Hastings House, New York, in 1946 (*Hastings House Americana*).

5. The Whitefield children were Edwin A. (presumably Albert), Wilfred, Cordelia, Constance, Rogwald, Edith, and another younger child. Graham Diet was a mid-nineteenth century fad, begun by vegetarian Sylvester Graham (1794–1851), who advocated a diet based on whole wheat flour.

6. "Galvanizing" is the term for a medical treatment which consisted of inducing an electric shock by means of a portable box with a crank; it was in use in the mid-nineteenth century for many ailments, physical and mental.

7. Lillian Stuart, who had emigrated to Canada from Blair Athol, Scotland, became the second Mrs. Whitefield. Whitefield evidently met her in Canada, possibly Adelaide, where he spent some time and purchased land shares.

8. *The Weekly Guide,* Port Hope, Sept. 11, 1858, supplied to the author by Mary Allodi of The Royal Ontario Museum. *Pioneer and Democrat,* St. Paul, Minn., August 17 and 21, 1858; *Minnesota Republican,* St. Paul, August 20, 27, 1858, footnoted in Bertha Heilbron's "Edwin Whitefield: Settlers' Artist," *Minnesota History,* 1966.

9. "Edwin Whitefield: Settlers' Artist," by Bertha L. Heilbron, in *Minnesota History,* published by the Minnesota Historical Society, St. Paul, vol. 40, number 2, 1966, pp. 62–77.

10. The area surrounding Kandotta had not yet been completely surveyed when Whitefield first saw it in 1856. On Colton's Township Map of the State of Minnesota, published in 1870, both Kandotta and the town of Whitefield are shown; but on Chapman's Sectional Map of the Surveyed Part of Minnesota, published two years later, neither Whitefield nor Kandotta nor Fairy Lake are shown. Just Lake Lillian, in southeast Kandiyohi County, remained.

11. Whitefield's well-written, lengthy obituary appeared in the *Boston Evening Transcript* on January 18, 1893.

12. The contract between Whitefield and the Heliotype Printing Company of Boston, Mass., on stationery from the Metropolitan Museum of Art, New York, the Office of the Secretary, March 6, 1883 (in Whitefield's hand): "I agree to color Heliotypes or Photographs, or make colored drawings of Two Hundred and Sixty Terra Cotta Vases, Pitchers, &c., to make

water-color Drawings of Eighty Glass Objects; One Hundred Bronze; One Hundred Gold or Silver; . . . all being a portion of the Cesnola Collection, contained in the Metropolitan Museum of Art, Central Park, New York City, for the sum of Fifteen Hundred Dollars, to be paid by the Heliotype Company of Boston, Mass. . . ." Donald Ramsay, whom Whitefield's daughter Lillian married before 1884, was a principal in the firm.

13. Heilbron, p. 75.

14. Whitefield's daughter Lillian was buried in Reading in 1915; his wife was buried under a Whitefield monument in an adjoining plot in 1923. Upon the death of the second daughter, Mabel, in 1951, Whitefield's body was removed from the cemetery in Dedham, Mass., to be buried with the rest of his immediate family. A granddaughter, Flora M. Ramsay, was buried there in 1965.

15. *Elementary Art, or, the Use of the Chalk and Lead Pencil advocated and explained,* by J. D. Harding, published in London by Day & Son, lithographers to the Queen, 4th ed., 1854. It also contains a portrait by Firth, which Whitefield copied, without attribution. It is to be found in the Whitefield collection at the Boston Public Library, bearing the comment, "The only attempt I ever made at a portrait."

16. George Warren Smith, printer and joiner in New York in the mid-1850's, a partner in the firm of Smith Brothers.

17. D. W. Moody (David), active in New York in the 1840's; drew views of Oswego, New York, and New Orleans for the Smith Brothers.

18. The three views of Brooklyn of interest here are:
View of Brooklyn, L.I. / From U.S. Hotel, New York.
   Drawn from Nature and on Stone by E. Whitefield.
      1846   15 x 36
Brooklyn, L.I.
   Lithograph by the Smith Brothers, printed by Endicott & Co., after a painting by J. W. Hill.
      1853   23½ x 39
Brooklyn, N.Y. 1854
   Extra large folio engraving by Wellstood and Peters after

B. F. Smith, Jr. Published by Smith, Fern & Co.
      1854   24 x 10

19. The Fern case is at the Hall of Records, New York City, #F-231.

20. The following page in a Whitefield diary gives an indication of the ratio of tinted to colored views:
Views left in Paris Mar. 1, 1857

Quebec	1 cold	12 tinted
Montreal	2	3
Kingston	—	20
Toronto	4	8
Hamilton	1	2
London	3	6
Ottawa	3	41
N. Falls	—	14

21. *Iconography of Manhattan Island,* Supplementary List of Prints, Drawings, etc., by I. N. Phelps Stokes (New York: Robert H. Dodd, 1918), vol. III, p. 894, no. 59.

22. Robert Hinshelwood, engraver, emigrated to America c. 1835; he drew illustrations for Schoolcraft's *Information respecting the . . . Indian Tribes of the United States,* 1849; a view of New York University; and illustrations for William Cullen Bryant's *Picturesque America,* 1872–74.

23. C. W. Burton was a competent artist, lithographer, and engraver working in New York in the mid-1800's. In 1849 he did a view of the Bay and the city of New York, with Brooklyn and Jersey City. According to *The New-York Historical Society's Dictionary of Artists,* he was possibly active in Boston at the same time.

24. A review of *Homes of our Forefathers in R.I. and Conn.,* published by the *Boston Journal,* April, 1882.

25. *Proceedings of the Massachusetts Historical Society,* vol. XIX, published by the Society, Boston, 1882.

26. The SPNEA recently received a sketchbook, too late for inclusion of the indicated ×'s. They now own original drawings for all but the following five: Whipple or Abbott House, Providence, R.I.; Coddington House, Newport, R.I.; Scovill or Johnson House, Waterbury; Old Tavern & Store, Bolton, Conn.; the Butler House, Wethersfield.

Bibliography

The main sources for this book were the diaries and other papers in the White-field collection at the Boston Public Library. Following is a summary of the years covered by the diaries: 1842; 1843 (May 30 to June 5); 1846; 1848 (to March); 1850; 1852–1853; 1855–1856; 1858; 1859; 1861 (June through August); 1866 (June through September); 1882–1883; and a few pages for 1888–1889.

Museums and historical societies visited were, in Massachusetts, the American Antiquarian Society, Archives of American Art, Boston Athenaeum, Museum of Fine Arts, Essex Institute, Fogg Museum and Robinson Hall at Harvard University, Merrimack Valley Textile Museum, and the Society for the Preservation of New England Antiquities. Also seen were the collections at the Mariners Museum, Newport News, Virginia; New York City Hall of Records, the New-York Historical Society, and the New York Public Library; and, in Canada, the Public Archives of Canada and the Canadiana Collection, Royal Ontario Museum, Toronto.

Allodi, Mary. "Chronology of Edwin Whitefield." Mimeographed. Toronto: Royal Ontario Museum, 1965.

Brown, Alexander Crosby. "Steamship Disasters in Nineteenth-Century American Lithographs." *The Magazine Antiques* 53 (1948): 208–210.

Chandler, Joseph Everett. *The Colonial House.* New York: Robert M. McBride & Co., 1916, p. 4.

Chapman's New Sectional Map of Minnesota. Published by Dyer & Pasmore. Philadelphia: L. B. Lippincott & Co., 1856.

Chapman's Sectional Map of the Surveyed Part of Minnesota. Milwaukee, Wisconsin: Silas Chapman, 1872.

Colton's Township Map of the State of Minnesota. New York: G. W. and C. B. Colton, 1870.

Cowdrey, Bartlett, ed. *National Academy of Design Exhibition Record, 1826–1860.* New York: Printed for the New-York Historical Society, 1943.

Cummings, Abbott Lowell. "The Society's collections [Society for the Preservation of New England Antiquities]." *The Magazine Antiques* 77 (1960): 469.

DeVolpi, Charles P., and Winkworth, P. S. *Montréal Recueil Iconographique.* Montreal: Dev-Sco Publications, Ltd., 1963.

Drepperd, Carl W. *Early American Prints.* New York and London: The Century Co., 1930.

Drury, John. "The City In A Garden. Chicago before the Fire of 1871." *The Magazine Antiques* 43 (1943): 66–69.

Garrett, Wendell D. "Figures and figureheads: The maritime collection at the State Street Bank and Trust Company." *The Magazine Antiques* 90 (1966): 816–823.

Groce, George C., and Wallace, David H. *The New-York Historical Society's Dictionary of Artists in America, 1564–1860.* New Haven: Yale University Press, 1957.

Harding, J. D. *Elementary Art, or, The Use of the Chalk and Lead Pencil advocated and explained.* London: Day and Son, Lithographers to the Queen. 4th edition, 1854. (First edition unavailable.)

Harper, J. Russell. *Early Painters and Engravers in Canada.* Toronto: 1970.

Heilbron, Bertha L. "Edwin Whitefield: Settlers' Artist." *Minnesota History* (St. Paul, Minn.: Published by the Society) 40 (1966): 62–77.

————, "Phantom Cities in a Promised Land." *American Heritage* 14 (1963): 52–57.

Hendrickson, A. H. "Complete History of Kandota." *Sauk Center* (Minn.) *Herald.* June 7, 1928, p. 7.

Jefferys, Charles W. *A Catalogue of the Sigmund Samuel Collection, Canadiana and Americana.* Toronto: The Ryerson Press, 1952.

Jordan, Philip D., ed. "Territorial Daguerreotypes. Rural Minnesota as seen by an Artist." *Minnesota History* (St. Paul, Minn.: Published by the Society) 30 (1949): 111–121.

Kane, Lucille M. "The Papers of John Harrington Stevens." *Minnesota History* (St. Paul, Minn.: Published by the Society) 34 (1954): 144.

Koke, Richard D. *A Checklist of the American Work of John Hill (1770–1850), Master of Aquatint.* New York: The New-York Historical Society, 1961.

Lucas, Fielding, Jr. *Lucas' Progressive Drawing Book. In Three Parts.* Baltimore, 1828.

Massachusetts Historical Society, Proceedings of the, 1881–1882 (Boston: Published by the Society) 19 (1882): 335.

McClinton, Katharine. "American Flower Lithographs." *The Magazine Antiques* 49 (1946): 361–363.

Metropolitan Museum of Art. The Terracottas and Pottery of the Cesnola Collection of Cypriote Antiquities. New York, 1895.

"Ohio's Historical Society." *The Magazine Antiques* 49 (1946): 64.

Peters, Harry T. *America on Stone.* Garden City: Doubleday, Doran and Company, Inc., 1931.

"Questions and Answers." *The Magazine Antiques* 7 (1925): 32.

Ramsay, John. "The American Scene in Lithograph." *The Magazine Antiques* 60 (1951): 180–183.

Rossiter, Henry P., ed. *Selections from the M. & M. Karolik Collection of American Water colors & Drawings, 1800–1875.* Boston: Museum of Fine Arts. 1962.

Scully, Vincent J., Jr. *Shingle Style.* New Haven: Yale University Press, 1955, p. 70 fn.

Spendlove, F. St. George. *The Face of Early Canada.* Toronto: The Ryerson Press, 1958.

Stokes, I. N. Phelps, and Haskell, Daniel C. *American Historical Prints, Early Views of American Cities, &c.* New York: New York Public Library, 1932.

Wainwright, Nicholas B. *Philadelphia in the Romantic Age of Lithography.* Philadelphia: Historical Society of Philadelphia, 1958.

Index

The Index basically consists of Whitefield's works referred to in the text and the geographical areas through which he traveled. Entries in capital letters refer to the numbered list of Whitefield's prints. Page numbers in italics refer to illustrations.